# SORRY, NOT SORRY

# SORRY, NOT SORRY

## Experiences of a brown woman in a white South Africa

### HAJI MOHAMED DAWJEE

PENGUIN BOOKS

Published by Penguin Books
an imprint of Penguin Random House South Africa (Pty) Ltd
Reg. No. 1953/000441/07
The Estuaries No. 4, Oxbow Crescent, Century Avenue, Century City, 7441
PO Box 1144, Cape Town, 8000, South Africa
www.penguinrandomhouse.co.za

Penguin
Random House
South Africa

First published 2018

1 3 5 7 9 10 8 6 4 2

Publication © Penguin Random House 2018
Text © Haji Mohamed Dawjee 2018

Cover photograph © Neo Baepi

PUBLISHER: Marlene Fryer
MANAGING EDITOR: Robert Plummer
EDITOR: Lauren Smith
PROOFREADER: Bronwen Maynier
COVER AND TEXT DESIGNER: Ryan Africa
TYPESETTER: Ryan Africa

Set in 11.5 pt on 16 pt Adobe Caslon

Printed by **novus print**, a Novus Holdings company

MIX
Paper from
responsible sources
FSC
www.fsc.org    FSC® C022948

Penguin Random House is committed to a sustainable future for
our business, our readers and our planet. This book is made
from Forest Stewardship Council ® certified paper.

ISBN 978-1-77609-266-6 (print)
ISBN 978-1-77609-267-3 (ePub)

*For my grandfather, who said:*
*People will steal the milk from your tea*
*But they cannot steal the knowledge from your mind*

# Contents

# Foreword

The other day, a young man proclaiming to be a 'woke white' asked me very nicely to be on his podcast, which sounded like an effort to teach other whites to be woke.

I was uncharacteristically sharp in my decline. 'Sorry, sir, but I think woke politics are fast asleep. Well, they certainly bore me to death.' Needless to say, the young man did not respond. I'm sorry for being the sharp matriarch I am determined not to be, but I was true to my view. In my experience, it can be a movement that excludes and punishes, speaking a language that bamboozles.

In its writing, it can often speak at and not to.

I'm in a phase of my writing that seeks to include, to tell stories and to find solutions, so I often find woke writing dense with didacticism but low on style. *Sorry, Not Sorry* upends my notions and has me alive, again, to the potential – it has woken me up and made me take a second look at the cultural and racial questioning essential to our time.

New political trends interest me and the self-proclaimed 'woke' generation are vital and interesting. Using social media as a mass urban medium, they are changing norms faster than my generation did with their digital smarts.

Take the film, *Inxeba* (*The Wound*). A love story that takes place in a Xhosa initiation school, it has set South Africa alight as traditionalists claw against the film. Some scaredy-cat movie houses cancelled screenings when a particularly forbidding woman from the hitherto unknown Icamagu Institute staged a sit-in at the Commission for the Promotion and Protection of the Rights of the Cultural, Religious and Linguistic Communities (the Orwellian flower in our bouquet of Chapter 9 institutions which protect and advance constitutional rights).

I've seen this show-reel before. Every time the SABC tried to screen a documentary on why so many young initiates were dying in the two initiation seasons, it would be hauled off the air as tradition clashed with transparency.

And I know, rather intimately, how freedom of artistic impression has been trumped by the rights to culture and religion: I'm the editor who published images of the prophet Muhammad and of *The Spear* painting by Brett Murray, and got damned for them.

We are a country that primes peace and stability over free expression (in an often false binary, I might add) and one that, until now, assumed the unassailable right to cultural and traditional protection, certainly over artistic production.

That changed with *Inxeba*, as the woke generation adopted the film and turned its screening into a cultural movement against being told what it could or could not watch.

So, I am in a season of new love with woke people. And Haji Mohamed Dawjee has enhanced my affection with this collection of touching, loving, incendiary, searing and intimate essays. She's both woke and funny, and she can write.

\* \* \*

One of the reasons I divorced woke politics (and it divorced me too, I have to be frank) is that it can often be tedious and insider. Also, I'm a non-racialist rainbow nation adherent, which is a bit of a profanity in that world. The language of woke can handicap. Take this. I work at *HuffPost SA*, the South African sister to the *Huffington Post* family. We write headlines snappily and quickly – I labelled something a politician did as 'dumb' and left.

The news editor called. 'Some people are complaining. Your language is ableist.'

'What?'

She explained that it could be read as a slur on people who couldn't speak. I was, well, dumbfounded. I still am when I get hit by phrases like 'cis-het normativity'. Come on, own up: you don't know what that means either.

There is none of that in Haji's screamingly funny, achingly painful, excoriatingly honest *Sorry, Not Sorry*. It's norm-challenging without the lazy descent into the rhetoric of slogan. It shows and doesn't tell, except at the very end, where the author explains the title.

I don't know where to begin to introduce you to the little pearls dotted in this first (but not last) book by Haji. So let's start at the top: an essay called 'We don't really write what we like' – a response, of course, to Steve Biko's *I Write What I Like*.

She starts: 'No one owns their stories and the telling of them like white male writers. They are given endless opportunities for it. They can write about anything. They can pen rants about white-men problems and white-men wealth. They can wax lyrical about cars and boats and spaceships ... the cherry on the vanilla cake is that they also get to write the soft, sensitive, soulful stuff.'

Such freedom, she notes, is not available to writers of colour: 'When was the last time you saw a piece of writing in mass-produced, commercial media by a person of colour who stitched together lengthy, breathtaking sentences about, let's say, a nostalgic song they happened to hear on the bus, or the train, or the aeroplane while on their way to deliver a handwritten note to an ex-lover they were trying to win back?'

And so, Haji writes.

She writes about tekkies, her grandpa, her mom and dad, a night at a pub. She writes about Serena Williams and her own aborted tennis career and she writes about her love for her wife.

Read it all, but if you dip in and out, make sure that you read 'A brain tumour can change your mind', the essay featuring the speech Haji's dad made at her wedding to the equally gifted journalist and writer Rebecca Davis. You will smile and dab away a tear for days. And while you're there, read about her 'anti-establishment' grandpa too. She makes his character come alive as he drives her to school in his olive-green Merc, and cooks exploding soup at their home in Laudium, Pretoria.

She writes what she likes. She writes about Bollywood movies, about tweeting Nelson Mandela's death, and she writes a journal about depression that is quite the best piece of mental-health writing I've read. In 'The curious case of the old white architect', she writes what a media establishment that Haji says is still white-dominated would not let her write, because it has pigeon-holes for what black women must write.

As a black woman writer only now starting to break out of my own pigeonholes, this book has been a guide. I've not felt the media establishment weight as Haji has, but mine has been self-imposed by my historical view that all art, all writing, had to serve the struggle for justice – there was to be no art for art's sake. This is not to say the anthology is not profoundly political.

It is. It is hard but compelling and often funny in its grappling
with South Africa's race politics.

\* \* \*

If I weren't afraid of catching it for days from her, I'd say Haji
was South Africa's answer to a young Salman Rushdie.

That's too glib, but her essays on religion are considered and
resonated with me. Haji was raised Muslim and is highly educated in the Islamic faith, so she goes toe-to-toe when bigotry
masquerades as a religion, but also celebrates when it is van-
quished.

Choosing a favourite essay is like trying to choose among all
the young journalists I read with such avid joy. They are all good,
but if you are interested, as I am, in female heroines, don't skip
her story of the Prophet's wives, Bibi Aisha and Khadija, in 'And
how the women of Islam did slay'.

Haji writes: 'Women in Islam have slayed (with the sword and
otherwise) for years. It's a fact. But these facts are secrets. Just
don't read the Quran properly, or delve into the research and
historical books, okay? Most Muslim people I know don't bother
anyway. They're afraid of seeing things they don't want to know.
Like how women have lots of rights and are just as entitled to
freedoms as men. But why trade in facts when you can trade in
the degradation and exploitation of women? Such fun.'

This set of essays will discomfort, and you will find yourself
shouting back at the author when she is particularly incendiary.
But you will come away edified and challenged and in touch
with a generation that questions shibboleths with charm and ease.

FERIAL HAFFAJEE

# We don't really write what we like

No one owns their stories and the telling of them like white male writers. They are given endless opportunities for it. They can write about anything. They can pen rants about white-men problems and white-men wealth. They can wax lyrical about cars and boats and spaceships. They can have reams and reams of motivational articles published about being 'bosses'. Without, mind you, ever having to refer to sexual harassment, unequal opportunities, discrimination or unequal pay. But the cherry on the vanilla cake is that they also get to write the soft, sensitive, soulful stuff. You know?

Like that time one of them – many of them, *all* of them – got paid to take a five-star hot air balloon across the universe until they reached the Northern Lights or whatever. It must be really nice that, over and above the aches and pains stuff, they get to scribble beautiful, elaborate stories neatly threaded with free trips and once-in-a-lifetime excursions. Wonderful experiences complete with decadent buffets. Charming. No lives of servitude here. No minds of servitude either. They are just out there, writing what they like. And media outlets cannot get enough of it.

Let's talk about Steve Biko for a second. In 1978, Biko's collection of essays, *I Write What I Like*, was published in South Africa. Penned between 1969 and 1972, it was prohibited from being published before that because … well, we all know why. The name of the book – now famous and regularly quoted – comes from the title under which he published his writing in the South African Student Organisation newsletter using the pen name Frank Talk.

Biko, founder of the Black Consciousness Movement, remains a powerful figure in South Africa. He was a courageous fighter against apartheid whose writing and insight is testament to not only his wisdom but also his passion and courage.

He is also extremely cool. Biko is so cool, man. He resonates because of his mind, but he is also relatable because he is so damn cool. That's why a lot of young people like him. Many of them have not even read *I Write What I Like*, but tons can emulate his vibe. I've met a few of these youths. A lot, actually. Biko's image endures. The way he lived and the way he died are romanticised, and in this time of youth rising and buildings falling, no revolutionary encompasses the iconic aesthetic of young heroism more than he does. His is an image of rock-star proportions neatly tied up with charisma. Today's youth may not have read the literature, but they have certainly adopted Biko's definitive image, which in Millennial terms can only be described as #radicalfleek.

The key precept in the Black Consciousness Movement can be summarised in one quote from said book: 'The most potent weapon in the hand of the oppressor is the mind of the oppressed.' This central tenet refers to the relationship between liberation and servitude. The quote extends beyond the physical properties of servitude and addresses mental slavery. It urges black people to own their stories, to break free from the shackles of predetermined narratives imposed on them by the people history 'belongs to'. It is a calculated statement. Firm in its determination to inspire black people to discover their own pasts, their own values and their own selves. And more importantly, it is a reminder that they must be the ones to own and tell of those discoveries. It's a powerful ideology, one that resonates with me when I think about writing what we like today.

But let's get back to basics. The second half of the Biko quote I cited above goes like this: 'So as a prelude whites must be made to realise that they are only human, not superior. Same with Blacks. They must be made to realise that they are also human, not inferior.'

Let's focus on the 'whites (think they) are superior' bit. How can we make whites realise that they are not superior but only human, and, in turn, how can we rise out of inferiority if we cannot tell superior stories? Even if we take ownership of our stories and claim the rights to them, we are still – in many instances – unable to paint the entire picture. Let's admit that we may write, but we definitely may not write just anything.

When was the last time you saw a piece of writing in mass-produced, commercial media by a person of colour who stitched together lengthy, breathtaking sentences about, let's say, a nostalgic song they happened to hear on the bus, or the train, or the aeroplane while on their way to deliver a handwritten note to an ex-lover they were trying to win back? Or what about reading a long-form essay by a person of colour who wrote a story about a story *about* a story they once heard about a great-aunt's kettle somehow discovered in a second-hand store, and in some strange way this kettle played a massive role in reuniting a pair of twins who were separated at birth? Or some crap … It could happen. These kinds of real-life experiences happen to white male writers all the time. I know this because they get to tell us about it.

They get published and they get paid and they get praised for stories like these. Stories that often have little point, except to entertain and inspire. Beautiful thoughts written by white men get published on full pages of weekly newspapers, or posted on websites to be shared until kingdom come. Simply because they were 'brave' enough to tell it. 'Brave' enough to spread joy and magic, and sprinkle fairy dust over the gravesite of news we're offered every day.

Dear public, this is not *brave*. This is opportunity. This is privilege. I am questioning, and have questioned for a long time, whether another pretty story about a white man's life is altogether necessary.

Their work need not contain stark revelations about race or religion or revolution. These kinds of stories are empty of confrontation and that's considered okay. They do not have to be educational. They need not investigate transformation and discrimination. There is no demand for factual statements of intersectional feminism, for example. There is no struggle in their sentences. All features, by the way, that must be present to the max in stories by people of colour. When last did you read a piece by someone who wasn't white that did not embody one or more of the aforementioned themes?

I am not saying we, as people of colour, should stay away from writing about the 'isms' and more. Baby Jesus, Moses and Muhammad know that if we don't write about those pressing and necessary issues, no one will. Or worse, the ones who *do* write about them will be the ones who have no claim to those stories. They do not own the experiences, and therefore, should not *write* the experiences. That would be filth and lies, although it happens nevertheless. We call it appropriation. It comes in many shapes and sizes.

We own the hard stuff. We really do. We own the struggles. And if we don't write about them, the country will forever dwell in the lily-white utopia that once was. If we do not claim and drive these conversations, we leave room for our minds to be colonised once more. But here's the truth (and strike me if you will): the struggle is exhausting. And we are not *just* the struggle. And so sometimes (by which I mean a lot but not *all* of the time), I wish I could get paid to write the nice stuff. Because, you know what? We also like nice things.

We too have nice experiences. We think about things and dream and have magic in us. We have fuzzy fables to share. But here is the other truth: no one cares about the wonders of a day in the life of a person of colour, how they felt when they saw that rainbow rise over the abandoned railway track in the middle of some small town. We even travel, you know. How come no one wants to know that? The readers are not interested and, more importantly, the editors are not interested. Isn't this a kind of oppression as well? To keep me down you must deny me my experience. Perpetuate the stereotypical narrative. People of colour are not allowed to have nice things. Those are reserved for whites.

Excuse me while I shed my modesty for a paragraph or two in the sharing of this here tale: I once wrote this gorgeous piece about India. My god, was it gorgeous. I went deep and then I went drippy and then I brought it all back with some real, hard truths about demographics and that sort of thing. In 1200 words or so, this story had everything. *Everything.* It was the kind of story that makes a reader weep, then think, then laugh, then weep some more, then dream, then think again. It was a thing of beauty. Real beauty. I submitted it everywhere. And that is where the paragraph of pride ends and the multiple paragraphs of humiliation begin.

I was insecure about my work. I had no white-superiority complex to speak of. My asking price for the story was R1.50 per word. A joke, really. I ended up getting nothing. First, because absolutely no one in South Africa wanted it, and second, because the US website that ended up publishing it was a contributor site and, well, they did not pay. I don't think I expected too much. In fact, I think my goals for the entire project were fairly standard grade. I failed. But you know who passes their writing goals with flying colours every single time? White men. Had a white dude written that piece, it would have been engraved on a platinum plaque and put on display for the entire world to see, because we simply *cannot* miss out on their stories.

Not so long ago, in fact, I read something similar. It was about India as well. White-man byline intact. Shouting at me. Loud. Proud. Aggressive. A firm reminder of my little place in the world. Or in the writing industry. My little space. Thank god for the media. Honestly, if they do not do their best to remind us of opportunity-discrimination I do not know who in the hell will. By the way, I know what you're thinking: *Just don't read it then*. Well, how would I ever have anything to write about and how would I ever get published if I didn't continue to torture myself with the harsh truths of a struggle? *Must pen struggle. Must keep it fresh. Only way to get published and make living.* Those words are on my bathroom mirror. Oh, by the way, we have mirrors.

But I digress. This India story. It paled in comparison to mine. Truly. To be honest, it paled in comparison to anything I have ever read about India, ever. Including those ridiculous, offensive Buzzfeed listicles white youth throw together when they are done finding themselves in Delhi. But there it stood on the website. Praised. Worshipped, even. Each comment underneath it a standing ovation. A public handjob. The majority of commenters were white. I often find it's this demographic who are most likely to have time to sign up on Disqus so they can post comments on websites. And troll people. They ate the India story up.

They devoured the part about the mud on the banks of the Ganges, how it felt and how it smelt. They sipped on the long, soothing sentence about the moon, and the light it threw over the dead Indian night in a small village too poor to afford the comforts of electricity. They swallowed whole the metaphor spewed out towards the end about the subcontinent's hot sun tearing through the polluted sky like a hurried surgeon slicing through a cadaver during an emergency research project. And then they laughed heartily at how the entire story had no point except to let everyone know that India sucks and the author is never returning. He could not pass up the opportunity to visit because of the silver platter it came on, but, he reiterated, India does suck.

Well, ain't life grand, buddy?

Again, I question whether the stories about the grandeur and the grand opportunities of buddy's life have any role to play.

They do not change my life in any deep, meaningful way. They do not challenge my disposition on political economy, race relations or cultural wisdom. Do they contribute to the discourse of a fractured country trying to sew itself up in a multitude of ways? No. But it must be said that, while they are meaningless, they sure are pretty. And let's be fair: it is nice to be distracted. In the deep winter of policy and principles and editorials and analyses, we need a seasonal change. Why not stop in the middle of reading all the other depressing stuff and smell the roses?

I will tell you this: I am so tired of smelling the same damn roses.

Do I want something beautiful to read? Absolutely. I just want to be able to write it as well. I want *us* to be able to write those stories. Those stories garnished with life's experiences. If escape is part of the journey of reading, then why is my only getaway through the eyes of white men? I also want to write about catching up with lost friends over warm cups of coffee in foreign places and have that be acceptable and 'newsworthy'. We too have souls to bare in a personal way that reveals how we love, regret and feel gratitude, among other things.

When I read these stories, the ones written by white men, the ones about their privileged lives, all I am reminded of is a beautiful lie made of hard truths. And when I start to pick apart not only the content but also the freedom to be able to write that way, ugly monsters start to surface: anger, envy and frustration at my comparatively limited opportunities. As a writer of colour, these monsters haunt me. They tear away at my self-esteem while I stick to something I'm more 'worthy' of writing, because there is no value in any of my other stories.

We talk about white privilege, we talk about entitlement and we talk about the complex intricacies of racial superiority and white power. We are aware of the imbalance of wealth distribution that results in inequality and selective opportunity. But this same privilege is not confined to economics and education and, and, and. White power is also creative liberty. And creative liberty means that if you want to write about the dewy flowers growing from the dry ground in the middle of the Mojave Desert, you can, as long as you fit the profile of white patriarchy. Because those are the ones who write what they like. They are free. They are not constrained by the shackles of literary servitude in the media industry.

We are. South African travel magazines, for example, don't have stories written by black women who were sent to Spain to eat a home-cooked meal on a mountain pass. Those little write-ups are few and far between, if they exist at all.

The only home-cooked meals writers of colour eat are the ones they make themselves in between trying to meet deadlines. Deadlines for pieces about things that are falling. Fees. Statues. Humpty Dumpty. I can't even listen to that Alicia Keys song any more. And I really like her. But everything is falling and we're all writing while the white dudes are flying. Flying from this side of the ocean to the other. The only travel vaccination they need? Immunisation from the manacles of responsible writing.

As a writer of colour, my opinion is forced to embrace a responsible theme – race, politics, equality, righteousness. I am constrained by needing to make some kind of point. I cannot write a column for a popular media organisation that details how many push-ups I did, or what song I sang in the shower. If I pitched a weekly column like that to a newspaper the response would be a hard no. No one cares. But ask me what lovely thing some white male saw on his Sunday walk the other day, and I will be able to tell you. The majority of news consumers will be able to tell you. Because that shit gets picked up. And they are good at it. I'm not saying they're not good writers. But I too would like to take a rocket to the clouds in my writing sometimes, instead of having to be on the frontlines of critical thinking.

There are, of course, the crowd-pleasers. The talking heads, painted in shades of brown and black. The writers of colour you sometimes find among the crowds at literary festivals. They aim to please. They agree with every white liberal on the panel. They soothe the crowds and make for easy listening by throwing pigeon crap (with their words) at the idea of cultural appropri-ation. They openly give permission to white writers to write about anything. 'Want to write in a black accent? ... Sure, go ahead. The fact that these things are out of bounds is bullshit.' They say stuff like this to the roaring applause of a majority white audience. And when they leave, they leave to write about the things they are allowed to write about as people of colour. Oppressed minds.

'So why don't you just do it? No one is stopping you,' you say. Well, I have. I have tried to break free before. There are times when I've crossed the border into that enchanting world of rainbows and I went ahead and wrote fun, leisurely columns. But instead of readers finding them charming or the column making someone's day better, I apparently made their day worse. I was blatantly told so. By any number of trolls.

The only way I can publish stories like these is by starting some lame blog no one is ever going to read because I am being too self-indulgent for a brown lady.

Biko has passed, but his truth has not. Here's some frank talk for you: why does it piss white people off so much when brown people are happy?

# A brain tumour can
# change your mind

My dad was not an easy father.

Guests once came to visit us for tea in Pretoria with their two young boys. These kids were out of control. When they left, my dad – burning to say something about their atrocious behaviour and lack of discipline – turned to my mom and said, 'We used to control our kids with our eyes.'

True story. Not a word had to be spoken. A look from my dad was all it took to set us straight.

I enjoyed a portion of my childhood, but I also spent a lot of time forgetting it. Many hours have been dedicated to erasing my father's expectations of me. Only four things mattered to him. The first was that we get an education, and always continue striving to get one. The second was that we be successful; academically outperforming everyone else was crucial. The third was that we find absolute financial independence.

And the fourth most important thing to my dad, or so it seemed to me, was that tasks be more difficult than I already found them. Relentless criticism seemed to be the order of the day, every day. His expectations, and his threshold for satisfaction, were so impossibly high that I would never meet them.

I tried. But failure stained all my efforts. And then, when I stopped trying, failure spilt into my lack of effort as well.

I used to think we didn't get much from my dad as kids. My grandfather provided spending money, toys and plenty of playtime. My dad was a behind-the-scenes dad. When he appeared for his cameo, he came with life lessons. Hard lessons. And a survival kit. He passed his survival kit around like a toolbox from which we could fashion our own hard shells. He had collected each piece of equipment through the course of his life and neatly packed them away to hand over to us as we grew up. We did not want these tools. They presented themselves in the form of lectures, reprimands and the silent treatment, to name a few. But what the tools ended up teaching us is invaluable.

He taught us to ask for nothing and work for everything. He erased the idea of entitlement from our hearts and minds. He enforced rules and regulations, not only to instil in us a sense of responsibility, but so that we knew to break them only if we could face the consequences with accountability. Because, in life, everything has consequences and we must be strong enough to face them in order to survive. And he hammered home his most important ideology: success is the biggest and best form of revenge.

My dad is a tough man. His life has made him resilient. His is a typical zero-to-hero story, but it's not run-of-the-mill. A boy from the slums of Marabastad managing to become a professor of orthodontics at the University of Pretoria is not an average narrative. It's the opposite. It's a plot thick with struggle and adversity. Each sentence heavy with overcoming: overcoming race, economics and social power. All these variables and more have made him a hard man.

There are many intermissions in the course of a life, and it's usually in those intermissions that we take a step back to collect our thoughts and compose ourselves. We take a moment to compile the notes in the margins of our lives and construct full sentences that give an account of our lives thus far.

What have we been up to? Where have we been? What do we have to repent for? Whom have we hurt and whom have we forgiven? What do we mean to the world, if anything? What do we mean to ourselves and what do we mean to the ones we love most? All questions whose answers make us who and what we are.

These intermissions can take the form of a job interview, a birthday or anniversary, the death of a parent or another close family member. They can even exist as that little space of time after you've ordered your drink and you're waiting for your food. All you have left to do is think. You take your intermission. You take stock.

And in some cases, the intermission is the chapter where you have a life-threatening illness.

It's at this period in his life that my dad closed one chapter so he could start another. So he could start another 'him'.

In Islam, death is not the end; it is only the beginning. Life in this world, with all its material inclusions, is a borrowed experience. It is an exam a Muslim must write for the reward of an eternal life. This world ends. The next goes on forever.

This is an important theme in Islamic theology. If a Muslim lives well, and has used their one chance on earth to prepare for an eternal life to come, death is only a transition. A bridge between the seen and the unseen universe. Death is nothing to fear, especially to the faithful and the righteous.

To those people, death is love. It arrives with affection and departs tenderly with their souls. To the faithful and righteous, the angel of death brings divine perfume and a shroud for the deceased. The last breath exits the body with pleasure into the angel's keeping and is taken to the seventh heaven.

In 2015 my dad was diagnosed with a brain tumour. He told us on Mother's Day. We were out for lunch and he just kind of slipped it in like it was no big deal. He played it down so much that I don't think we grasped its seriousness until my mom shared the symptoms he'd been experiencing for some time. He was going deaf in one ear. He got dizzy occasionally and had started to bump his car on kerbs and pillars, or veer off the road. His balance was completely off so it affected his eyesight. He was hallucinating.

The tumour wasn't a little thing. It was a big thing. As big as a golf ball, in fact, and it sat on a web of nerves in the lower portion of his brain. Just waiting for tee off by a neurosurgeon.

There is nothing more frightening for a child than to sit face-to-face with your father, who looks perfectly healthy, while he picks apart his own last will and testament with you the night before life-threatening surgery. There is nothing more frightening than looking into the desperate face of your mother, whose eyes are begging for some semblance of understanding. The last thing on her mind? Administration.

My sister took notes. She jotted down details of where things were stored, what passwords unlocked which files, which family member we could trust to ask for help in an emergency.

My brother made mental notes of timelines. A will is a document that arrives after death and lives for a long time after someone has passed, especially if the person's life was as full as my dad's. He is wealthy with knowledge and experience and security. My brother also asked the important questions. He went digging for answers to questions we didn't know needed answering.

Me? I sat mute, listening. My ears tied up with the talking happening around me, my thoughts prisoner to what I was hearing. The reading of my father's will scared me more than the news of the tumour. Today he was reciting that will in his own voice; tomorrow his speech might be a memory. The survival rate for the surgery wasn't high.

A part of me prayed for ease. I have a healthy relationship with death. My relationship with loss, however, is less secure. To manage that emptiness I filled the space with a thought I still feel guilty about: *Perhaps, when he passes, I can live a life out of the closet without the fear of disappointing him.*

To be clear, I would choose a life of secrecy over losing my father. Still, when death is about to close a door, all kinds of strange comforts come in through the window. The idea of avoiding the same degree of disapproval I evoked in him as a child brought me some kind of relief, and I figured that perhaps he could die in peace without knowing I was gay, our relationship intact.

The Quran doesn't say much about homosexuality. Religious texts as a whole assume a theme of heteronormativity. In fact, in Judaism, Christianity and Islam there is only one central story that relates to a traditional condemnation of homosexuality. Male homosexuality, to be more specific. And that is the story of Sodom. What conservatives forget is that this story is not about love or consensual sex at all. It is about rape and inhospitality.

One night, a mob gathers outside the house of Lot (Lut in Arabic) and demands access to Lot's visitors, who we have come to interpret (in all three religions) as male. The mob wants to rape them as a punishment for suspected espionage. To maintain both his status as a good host and the trust of his guests, Lot offers the mob his two virgin daughters instead. Perhaps he considers the rape of his daughters a lesser evil than the rape of his male guests. Raping a woman, it seems, is somehow more permissible than raping a man.

The story's reference to actual homosexuality is unclear, yet it is used to prove its sinfulness in all circumstances. It's because of the propagation of confused sermons like these that believers often find themselves discarding portions of the population based on whom they choose to love.

This was my fear. I had enough experience of my father's thinking, the map of his mind, to know that telling him his daughter was a sinner was no throwaway statement. The only thing in danger of being thrown away was me. I was not ready. In this way, living (in Islam) is more unsettling than dying.

But illness is change, by its very nature. It sees the body morph into something different. It pushes the physiology of its victim to an unthinkable edge. And at that edge, where the ill are faced with either falling or turning back and walking away, values start to change. The things that matter come alive and the things you have yet to figure out start to surface. There is a new appreciation and respect for time. The figuring out starts to happen very quickly. Any time left to spare is safeguarded for the moments you will need it most. For when you will need mere seconds to change your point of view on something, or for that short moment you have to say 'goodbye' or 'I'm sorry'. And while you stand there, you play everything back to yourself. You see the scene where you say goodbye. You wish you didn't have to, but you have little choice in that matter.

The apology bit? Well, you decide that if you turn from

that edge and leave the illness behind, you will never again put yourself in a position to ponder an apology. You will always say sorry.

There are endings in death even if you think of it as a beginning. But how you navigate your illness decides the nature of that end. Will you leave feeling good or bad? Will you leave full or empty?

When my dad lay in his hospital bed the night before his operation he was in good spirits. He found comfort in the things he knew and he made peace with the things he didn't. We gathered around him. I made the odd joke and everyone laughed. And then we had to say goodbye. We didn't know whom we would see the next day or if we would see him again at all. I can remember wondering how I was going to feel if all I had left, twenty-four hours later, was a piece of paper he read to us the day before. His words left behind. His voice gone. We kissed and hugged him. Told him we loved him. Mary, my sister, started to cry. Her tears felt like they fell inside of me, a dark well of quiet emotions. I told her everything would be okay.

People always say a near-death experience brings with it some kind of interaction with a light. A glimpse of heaven. A peaceful alleyway between life and death. Some who have survived a coma or a long surgery talk about their lives flashing before their eyes. Seeing a montage of memories, a visual autobiography. I don't know whether my dad experienced this or not. I never asked. He must have. As a spiritual person, thoughts of heaven and letting go of this world could not have been far from his mind while he was anaesthetised for over nine hours. He didn't stay in that state of endless sleep though; he woke up. His soul returned to his body and I know that when it entered it did so in a rather abrupt way. Scientifically, there was some confusion in the 'awakening' process in theatre. It wasn't a gradual emergence so much as a shove back to the planet.

My dad's a soldier. He has overcome. He was once willing to let his children see him as the 'enemy' so that we could learn to overcome too – and we did.

In 2015 he overcame again. He beat a brain tumour and changed his mind. The 'enemy' left us and someone else took his place. Someone we feared less and loved more.

I was so sure of this that in October of 2016 I dropped him an email with few words and many truths. I told him I was engaged to a woman I loved. We were going to get married in December. I said, 'I have lived without the security of our relationship before. It will be hard, but if I need to, I must be okay with the fact that I might have to do it again.' He responded by saying he didn't know what to say just yet.

Two monthls later, my dad gave this speech at our wedding:

Assalamualaikum, good evening, molo, namaste.

Haji, Rebecca, honoured guests, family and friends.

It is indeed a great honour for us (my wife Gori and I) to be sharing this wonderful occasion with you.

As my family will attest, I am not one for long speeches. Life is short and there is much to do. Frankly, I am really no good at public speaking.

My interpretation of life is that it is analogous to a game, and in any game one needs to know and understand the rules. For it is in knowing the rules that one can challenge and rewrite them.

No rules were transgressed, trespassed or breached here today.

Instead, a lesson should be taken from this testimony of

love as to how honest and beautiful the rules of life can be when sincerely applied.

In my line of work, we act on scientific proof. We are trained not to prescribe any treatment that does not have any evidence of benefit. An interesting antidote to this paradigm that I came across in the movie *The Man Who Knew Infinity* is – and I quote – 'There are no proofs nor underlying laws that can determine the outcome of matters of the heart.'

Love is love.

We are because of love. We live by it. And we shall return to it.

Society can be fragmented in so many ways but in the end it is love and friendship that hold us all together.

Congratulations Rebecca and Haji. I wish you all the happiness in the world and love you both dearly.

Just as you have today rekindled the true meaning of the rule of love, I have no doubt that you will strive in your writing and your influence to free society from its blind adherence to dogma in favour of righteousness.

May Allah bless you both.


Hadiths report that the prophet Muhammad said: 'When the soul is taken out, the eyesight soon follows.' But what about when death tricks you instead of taking you? What about when you have a brain tumour and death treats your soul to a walk and shows you a little bit of light and a little bit of love? Perhaps when your soul returns and your eyesight along with it, you start to see things differently?

It could happen. It did.

# Don't touch me on my tekkies

Do you know what 'can't gets' are? They're one-of-a-kind, unique, special-edition sneakers that no one else has, because you just can't get them. To me, 'can't gets' are more than a single release of a shoe. My personal sneaker-Everest, my 'can't gets', are Nike Air Jordans. My friend Stephie and I often joke that one day when we get a pair of Jordans, we'll have made it in life. Every now and then I send her a picture just to remind her that the dream isn't dead. There's a pair of size fours out there waiting for us. And one day, we're going to walk into a store and drop cold hard cash on the counter without feeling guilty about where that money should have gone and we're going to walk out with our 'can't gets'.

It seems like a small, fickle goal, but it means everything. It's ambition, it's pride, it's having what you could never have and knowing that you're going to have it because you earned it. A lot of people don't understand that. Do you know how many times I get asked why expensive sneakers are so important to brown people? Because there comes a point in time when things like sneakers *can* be important. There comes a point when our feet deserve to wear the nice things our eyes stared at as kids. Don't touch me on my tekkies.

There's a recipe for washing white Converse All Stars. First, you need a bucket filled with warm water and some bleach – the kind that doesn't make the colour run. Add some washing powder and mix it all up. Give it a good swish so the powder starts to bubble. Then soak your shoes. Once the water has penetrated the canvas, grab an old-fashioned, dependable bar of green Sunlight soap. Scrub one shoe at a time using a small nailbrush so you can get between the grains of the laces and that hard-to-reach place where the rubber sole meets the shoe. Concentrate on one area at a time.

I usually start at the toe then work my way around the border of the shoe before lathering a healthy dose of soap on the underside and giving that a good scrub as well. All the while, the hand not doing the scrubbing is balled in a fist inside the shoe. Then I focus on the canvas. I scrub each side repeatedly, re-soaping each time. Once the sides are done, I undo the laces and give the tongue a thorough scour. After each helping of soap and the working of each patch of canvas, it's important to dip the shoe into the bucket to get rid of the green remnants of soap. There's always a danger that the tinge will stay behind if you don't. Once you're done, leave the shoe in the same bucket for what I like to call a 'safety soak' and start on the other one. When both shoes are spotless, leave them in the bucket to marinate while you work the laces methodically in much the same way.

Use your index finger and thumb and run them up and down each lace while it's soapy to make certain you get an even spread of suds, then pop them in the bucket as well.

While the laces soak, go ahead and give your shoes a rinse. Squeeze the soap out and rinse repeatedly until the remaining water drips clean, then slap the shoes together to shake off excess moisture. You can dry the shoes and the laces separately, or lace up and dry in a composed fashion. My preference is for the latter.

And now, here's the ultimate secret to maintaining pristine whiteness: give the shoe a liberal dusting of baby powder (the more expensive option), Maizena (the mid-range option) or plain old mielie meal (the classic option). Massage your powder of choice into the shoe, including the rubber trimming. Make sure to get it into the important seam areas and then leave your All Stars in the sun to dry. A word of warning: if you're using mielie meal I recommend drying your tekkies in the shade. The sun may turn the powder yellow and this can stain and ruin the shoe.

There are two reasons for maintaining the pallor of your white Converse All Stars. One: it always looks like you have a new pair of shoes. Two: longevity. If you take care of your All Stars properly, they remain wear-ready and comfortable for ages, preventing additional spending on new shoes for years to come.

The longest time I have ever kept a pair was twelve years. That pair was navy blue, but I followed the same cleaning recipe, minus the bleach, of course.

It was a sad day when I had to replace them. They saw me through both undergrad and postgrad degrees. They walked me in and out of school at my first real job. They dragged me through Europe and a couple of places in Asia. They saw Everest from the hills in Darjeeling and sweated their way through Goa. They trudged their way across the cobbled paths of Nottingham when I worked in a store – illegally. That pair of shoes journeyed across twelve years' worth of my life experience. They followed more roads than a global nomad and kicked the sand and grass in more parks than a ranger.

Until I had to replace that pair in December 2016 I never paid more than R200 or R300 for Converse. You can imagine my shock and disappointment when the new pair cost me R700. Then it struck me: Converse is the shoe equivalent of gentrification.

Tsotsi shoes. That's what they used to call Converse in white communities. I cannot count the number of times teachers commented on my feet when I wore them to civvies days. They told me I shouldn't wear them because they were the shoes of criminals. Converse were never white people's shoes. In their eyes, Converse All Stars were the shoes of the other and that's exactly what they saw every time they turned on the television or took a wrong turn on their way to safe suburbia. And with the sight of these shoes on the wrong feet, came all kinds of tsotsi conclusions.

To us, these tekkies were never a problem.

Converse All Stars were not tsotsi shoes. They were the symbol of a lifestyle; Converse meant you belonged to a certain community. And if you took care of them, you always had something to be proud of, no matter what. They were top of the range when compared to other tekkies at the time, but still relatively affordable. And the extra rands were worth it because of the shoe's quality and the length of time you would be able to wear them for.

To us, these tekkies were never a problem.

And they weren't a problem to the white person until they entered their communities on brown feet. Then all that changed. The tekkies started showing up in suburbs, they started showing up in places where there were hardly any people of colour. The rock clubs, the skateboarding communities of Cape Town, the coffee shops of Parkhurst ... You get the idea. In the past, I would enter these environments and get nothing but judgemental stares. Then things changed. The culture of Converse changed. The vibe changed.

To white people, these tekkies weren't a problem. Any more.

The best way to destroy part of a culture, even if that part is as material as a pair of shoes, is to take it from its people.

The power of white people to take things never dies, but our ability to access the things that once belonged to us suffers endless extinction. Even as a middle-class person of colour, R700 is a hefty price to pay for a pair of shoes that saw me and a generation before me through life. And now we pay the price of a people who have always wanted us to do the things they want us to do in order to be accepted. Not recognised. Just accepted. In other words, it's now acceptable for people of colour to wear All Stars because white people wear them, while the rightful owners of that trend go unrecognised.

Globally, a sneaker is more than a sneaker. This special breed of footwear stretches beyond its athletic purpose. It is an ideology. It conveys an identity, a class, a race. It has meaning. It has method. And the status of tekkie culture is no different in South Africa. The tekkie is a canvas for a specific, politicised point of view. The Converse All Star tekkie was a specific, politicised point of view.

But its canvas has been washed clean with the brush of plain old shallow fashion. Appropriation. The surface of the shoe demarcated and declared gentrified. Its meaning forgotten. Its space occupied by something else. The Converse All Star's political point of view has been silenced by white feet. No more will the shoe share a dialogue with people of the same community, who often had to whisper their thoughts to each other. A certain type of tekkie, like the All Star in South Africa, is a magnet that both draws a people together and sets them apart.

Our people were the progenitors of the Converse All Star. Our people. The kind of people who grew up in the designated locations of the Group Areas Act. It was the shoe of choice for the economically deprived. Selected because of its functionality, comfort and durability. Selected because of the sense of pride that came with all of that. But now, tekkie culture and its growing popularity on the other side of the privilege border create a further political divide – a culture war of sorts, between those who work hard to own and those who can afford to just … take.

A sneaker is not just a shoe. It's that point where childhood desperation and adult aspiration meet. It's where those two qualities kiss and touch and promise to become something new. A sneaker is not just a shoe. It is the difference between wanting and having. It is the running towards something instead of running away. A sneaker is not just a shoe. A sneaker is the difference between having and craving. It's that silent play that happens in your heart when it speaks of getting the things you need versus getting the things you want.

Philosophers have teased us with a riddle through the ages: if a tree falls in the forest with no one to hear, does it make a sound? The riddle is an existential conundrum that can and has been massaged into many meanings, the most popular being that sound is a product of the ears. If ears are absent, so is the sound.

But let's try another angle: that the riddle's main question is not about sound, but rather about loss. The loss of meaning. The loss between what something is and how it appears to be. And to many, *that* is the most important topic that can be extracted from this conundrum. The discord between the perception of something and how it really is. It's the difference between wearing shoes and wearing a declaration, and understanding the difference between the two. The meaning of something does not cease to exist just because someone is unaware of it.

A sneaker is not just a shoe. It is a statement. Is anyone listening?

When a tekkie shouts, will you know what it's saying when you don't bother to understand its language?

# Jane of all trades, master of none

Serena Williams is the best tennis player ever. The greatest of all time of everything. The GOAT. Serena Williams has never shied away from taking a strong position on sexism, body shaming or racism, to name a few. Serena Williams is my hero. I worship her. And yes, it's because she's so hardcore, but it's also because she does me a personal favour every time she wins at anything. Even if that thing is featuring in an awesome Beats by Dre headphones ad. Her sister, Venus, didn't appeal to me much. She lacked a spirit animal, a fighting tiger that raised its head to roar, the way Serena's so often did.

My childhood afternoons were filled with more extramural activities than I can count. Tennis was one of them. I'm not complaining; I was exposed to more opportunities than any of my friends at the time. The idea was that these acquired skills would give me future prospects, so I learnt a bunch of things that might come in handy some day.

Some of my 'future investment' activities were short-lived. Ballet, for example, as well as gala swimming at the gym and guitar lessons – not at the gym. But when I say short-lived, I don't mean they lasted a month or two. Oh no; in my family, when you start something, you finish it. Short-lived meant taking lessons for a couple of years, until you knew enough to carry on teaching yourself. I never did ballet ever again. I still mess about with the guitar – it's a great social instrument to play at hangouts, so that was a good investment, I guess – and as I've got older, swimming pools have become way too cold for my liking. I literally need them to be a hot bath before I get in. Having said that, I hate baths and prefer showers.

Another one of these activities was horse-riding. Man, can I *ry 'n perdjie*. So if ever shit goes down in the Wild West, I will be able to get away provided I have a good saddle, bridle, crop and fancy equestrian hat. Which makes horse-riding extremely boring, to be honest, and since I will never need to escape bank robbers in the Wild West, it also makes it unnecessary. I was never going to be a pretty *poppie* with a long, gorgeous plait flowing from my velvet headgear while I participated in dressage.

It was driving out to the lessons and the awkwardness of the whole situation that disturbed me more than those awful jodhpurs and riding hat. Every Wednesday, my mom would load my sister and me into her white Toyota Conquest and transport us from Laudium to the outbacks of Pretoria for an hour-long lesson with Eleanor and her son, Ben. Ben was no older than I was – twelve, possibly younger – and he rode a prize pony with a funky fringe. His mom owned the stables and the shires and most of the horses and the quaint little house at the top of the hill. It was charming, all of it. Very privileged and very charming.

I was awkward, brown, less experienced than this white kid with his Spartan horse, and very self-conscious of those tight pants I had to wear. I basically sucked at every minute of it. And I was well aware of the fact that my sister and I were being spoken to rather differently than white students. They were engaged with like the humans they were, whereas I always felt like we were being addressed as though we might be a little stupid or slow. I didn't know what this meant back then, but boy, do I know now. Anyway, I hated it, but I never expressed my dislike because I realised what hard work it took for my dad to be able to send us to these lessons. No one else who looked, walked and talked like us was doing it. The opportunity had never been available to my parents to begin with. I was grateful, still am. Also, in my family, one knew better than to deny or oppose any kind of education. Disobedience was an open initiation to a *vet klap*.

But I would like to moan about one thing here: I swear, I always got the oldest, biggest, laziest horse. Those white kids got some poster-worthy equines. This did not add any love to the equation (or equestrian, for that matter). A part of me still believes learning to ride a horse was a political point that my dad was trying to make – if white people could do it, so could we. True, right? Why the hell not.

The tennis lessons, I think, were less political. The idea was born of an observation in a tiny passage at our childhood home in Laudium. I was bouncing a found tennis ball with a broomstick. Mad skills, I tell you. Mad. My dad noticed and decided these mad skills were deserving of an actual tennis racquet and lessons. It was the most fun I ever had in my whole life. It was the only extramural I looked forward to. Running around in the sun, playing the occasional round robin and participating in tournaments organised by our then coach Jennifer – rumoured to be a former South African player. I was going to be a professional, luminous-yellow-ball buster. A completely unrealistic ambition in retrospect, now that I know how the world works. My sister and I were once again the only kids of colour at our lessons.

I didn't think about what this meant at the time. The meaning of it now does not bode well.

There were no players of colour on the pro-circuit either. Not that I recall; Top Sport certainly didn't broadcast any of their matches if there were. We were, however, blessed with strong women like Martina Navratilova and Steffi Graf. Steffi's game was always cautious and measured and guaranteed of a win, but I loved Martina more. Win or lose, she kicked ass and took names. And then all of a sudden their careers on the court died, just like my dreams, and that was that. Still, I thought that maybe I could one day be the coffee-coloured star in the Milky Way of white women tennis players.

When we weren't going for this lesson or that, we had to sit at home and do extra maths. Instamaths, to be specific. Instamaths is a collection of rectangular books that come in different levels and colours. Oh, the joy of solving problem after problem. Every time my dad came home with a new booklet for my sister and me, he acted like it was Christmas morning. Who needs toys when you can have recycled paper filled with numbers? I feigned enthusiasm; they were gifts, after all, and I did not want to seem bratty. But I still want to throw up at the thought of it. I'm pretty sure, though, that my sister, who is a lot smarter than me, was sincere in her delight.

Obviously these books landed on the same pile of useless efforts I have amassed since. I was no better at maths than any other extramural. I still needed extra maths tutoring all through high school. My Instamaths days in adolescence counted for nothing and one day I will reimburse my dad for all that money. Not today, though: first I will make up for all that time wasted when I could have been training to be a professional tennis player. The one thing I thought I could be really, really good at.

I didn't want to be a mathematician. I didn't even like school. I hated it. I'm pretty sure going to school is responsible for my certified depression. I wanted to bash balls and be a bloody star. This seemed like a realistic dream to me. More realistic than being a rosette-wearing equestrian or toe-tortured ballerina. Far-fetched, I know. The headline was never going to read: Little Girl from Laudium with the Big Backhand. People from Laudium didn't do anything really. Kids waited until they were a certain age, then got married. Before that, they cruised the streets in their parents' cars looking for people to marry. The Dawjee household operated differently. We did our sums and comprehension practice and played the piano. Watching *Egoli* to perfect our Afrikaans was considered a treat. Tennis seemed to fit perfectly with my abilities. It required fitness, a strong arm, a good pair of eyes and excellent coordination. It did not require an exceptional intellect. There were no report cards for tennis, and no exams (in the formal sense). I could do this, I thought.

But then piano lessons started eating into everything. They came with biannual printouts from the Trinity College of Music, showing results that once again paled in comparison to my exceptional sister's. And before you knew it, I was several sad certificates in and fifteen years old, too old to even think of going pro on the court. Then, one piano teacher's death and a few more sad reports later, I was seventeen – basically part of the geriatric society in professional tennis. Goodbye Wimbledon, hello strawberries and cream and religious Centre Court viewing on TV every winter. Even though I enjoyed playing the piano immensely, the bitterness of never being able to walk onto a lawn court sometimes washed over me like Jeyes Fluid, strong and nauseating. Piano lessons are where tennis champions go to die. Such was the dramatic disposition of a naive child. Torture, I know – playing the piano instead of tennis.

Even though I was still a dedicated Wimbledon watcher, I followed the women's circuit less and less. No one there understood my story or looked like me. No one could put themselves into the feelings of a young, silly brown girl from a formerly declared township. I became a Sampras fan, because it was easier to have a crush than to try to relate to anything. When Federer started playing and made Sampras old news, I hated him – I hated change. The retiring of a player only reminded me of my own dream deferred. (Now I want Federer to have my babies.) Still, I wondered, where was my superwoman?

Enter Serena Williams. She started playing and the broadcasts started changing. Her story was kind of like my story. Young teen, female. Dedicated dad, pushy but for good reason, wants his kids to be the best, etc. I knew this story. I mean, I didn't know it in a 'Gatorade wants to give me millions because I am so awesome' kind of way, but I knew it. So I packed away my sadness and released my inner Serena. I didn't make it, but she did and when she plays, I win.

This woman is literally a dream come true, and so now, every time I watch her, I'm reminded that she's living what was once my potential reality too. Every time Serena Williams wins, she triumphs for me, the girl who was learning how to suck at her eight-times table and playing scales instead of practising her drop shot.

Malcolm Gladwell says it takes 10 000 hours to become an expert at something. That's approximately three hours per day, every single day for 9.13 years. This leaves people like me with very little chance of being great at anything so late in life. Gladwell's theory has since been questioned because studies have found that the number of hours varies between domains. For example, practising boardgames or videogames for 10 000 hours will not necessarily make you an expert in the same way that practising some sports for 10 000 hours will.

But when it comes to tennis, the theory rings true. Deliberate practice is a predictor of success in fields that have super-stable structures, like tennis. When the rules of the game remain the same, you can master them. In less-stable fields, such as music, more practice does not necessarily amount to more skill. In fact, 21 per cent less than 10 000 hours is more than enough. *If* you have a natural gift. Ringo Starr drummed his ass off with the Beatles and remained a terrible drummer.

Maths, like music, is defined as significantly unstructured. I know this makes absolutely no sense because it's all organised with its theorems and formulas. But I'm not talking about algebra and calculus here, which themselves – while structured – are just concept upon concept upon concept. I am talking about advanced mathematics. The type of thing people assume you can do if you practise book after book of Instamaths – which is never actually going to be possible, because advanced mathematics, just like theoretical physics, has no structure whatsoever, and is completely abstract and disconnected from reality. Even though it feels like I lost hours of my life practising maths, I was never going to master it because I have no natural disposition for or interest in it. Being a concert pianist was a complete no-go even though I went ahead and got a music degree at the University of Pretoria. Tennis, according to Gladwell's theory, remains my only hope – but only if I can turn back the clock and redeem my 10 000 hours.

I take full responsibility for the fact that out of the million activities I had to do, I wasn't spectacular enough at any of them to even think of dedicating that much time to them. The maths thing paid off for my sister: she is amazing at science and any-thing numbers-related, and she's put it to good use by becoming a medical professional. My brother dedicated most of his life to the saxophone and he's a real, actual musician, and has probably amassed well over 10 000 hours now, even though he is six years younger than I am. Me? I find solace in the time that Serena's put in. Because she's the master of her trade to the Jane of my none, and she is definitely the hero to my zero.

# Begging to be white?

The global map suffocates me, and not by accident. It is an intentional asphyxiation. We can move from place to place to avoid the white privilege that surrounds us, but our strangulation is inevitable. It encloses. It meets us at the bank, it seats us at restaurants, it talks to us on the radio, it plays in front of us on television and it stares at us in print. The 'whites only' signs have been removed, but destroying physical evidence means nothing when the ideologies have stayed behind and continue to be recycled.

They're a constant reminder of a race we're meant to run, every day. Our lane is filled with hurdles. White people compete too, but in their lane it's a relay. Each one of them runs a shorter distance and leans on a system of support to guarantee consecutive wins. We've been subjected to a crippling variety of disadvantages from the beginning. And the race remains challenging. Mostly because equality is inconceivable and discrimination doesn't need a lot of imagination. It never has.

In her book *Americanah*, Nigerian author Chimamanda Ngozi Adichie writes about the difference in racial awareness between white people and black people: 'Race doesn't really exist for you because it has never been a barrier. Black folks don't have that choice.' There is so much truth in this. When last did you live a day without thinking about the colour of your skin and how you would be treated because of it at any moment? This is not a comment on a lack of pride or ownership of identity. Just because this awareness lingers in the back of our minds does not mean we're not proud of who we are. Now, how many times a day would you think about the colour of your skin if you were white? Never.

I often wonder what it would feel like to move through the world as a white person. Actually, that's a lie. I know what it would feel like: easy. It would be so simple. The rules would be my own. The consequences of my actions minimal. My ambitions would be my own as well. They would not be a product of this incessant need to prove myself. I could have as little or as much ambition as I wanted. I would owe the world nothing, yet benefit from the hard work of everyone else. I would carry great pride and no guilt. Entitled to a fundamental right. That right would be power. An embedded kind of power. Its existence established long before my grand entry into the world, its endurance seemingly eternal. I could be as negligent as I wanted, bathe in my own ignorance and have little to complain about, but complain nonetheless just because I could. Now isn't that a charming little universe?

I've given it some thought and here's what I would do in that charming universe.

### I would walk around barefoot

Not bothering to put shoes on would be a great timesaver. And prancing around in your bare hooves is a great cost saver. When white people don't bother with shoes in public, they're never judged for it. If I stood in the pasta-sauce aisle at a fancy grocery store as my authentic self, bare heels firmly on the ground, a lot of people would be physically disgusted.

It's economics. And it's racism. A shoeless person of colour in a fancy grocery store surely does not belong there and is probably trying to steal. But white people can go forth and conquer without shoes. I've even seen a white person shopping barefoot in Hyde Park, a fancy marble-laden shopping centre in Johannesburg. This person was not buying shoes, obviously. If I were white and didn't have to bother with the cost of shoes, I would also shop at Hyde Park a lot more.

## I would always ask to speak to the owner

You know what happens when I go shopping? I throw a lot of money away. Why? Just to prove I can. I can't even count the number of times I have been harassed and stalked by store attendants because of the assumption that I could not afford their clothes. So what do I do? Stuff like this: 'Give me one in every single colour.'

'Are you sure you want the 100ml Dolce & Gabbana? Have you looked at the price … ma'am?'

'Yes, I am sure. I will also take 100ml of the Versace, the Armani and the Hermès. I feel like the French deserve my money too. Thank you kindly.'

Now, if I ever encountered that degree of churlish behaviour while shopping as a white person (it never happens to white people, but bear with me), I would – instead of blowing cash – always ask to see the owner of the store. Why? Because she or he is going to be one of my tribe. I would have the confidence to do that. I would be so sure that the white owner would demand I be treated with respect. I would probably get an apology, and a free 100ml bottle of perfume over and above the discount I'd receive on the bottle I was willing to pay for. Most of all, my skin colour would automatically make my money more welcome and reaffirm my platinum financial status.

### I would own an empire of socks ... or something

Do you know how much it costs to rent a store in an upmarket mall with marble flooring and pillars made of blood diamonds? Do you know how much profit you have to make selling socks (for example) to pay that rent? White people do, and they don't have to care about it.

If I were white I would open one of these sock businesses. And when I say one, I mean at least one store in each province. White people aren't rich. They are wealthy. They have something called generational wealth.

Generational wealth means I would never have to worry about 'risk in the hope of profit'. My sock or hankie or 'single gloves for the left-handed man' business would thrive because my generational wealth would see to the fact that everything is paid for upfront, no debts. And after all the start-up costs, I would still have money left over for further expansion. Mostly, I would have fat stacks left over to make everything look cool. My shit would look swanky as hell, and everyone would trust the quality of my products because I was white.

### I would embrace trends like boho-chic

I've been told on one or two occasions that my general style can be described as 'heroin chic'. I think that mostly has to do with the fact that I never make an effort to pair things and I'm a bad sleeper so I always have dark rings under my eyes. It's an involuntary style, really.

If I were white though, I would embrace trends like these

intentionally. Like the boho-chic trend, for example. I would boho-chic my way through life so hard without ever having to worry about the fact that I look poor. I would totally pull off boho-chic, hobo-chic and vintage-retro-postmodern-vagrant-sartorial-fleek (or whatever else is cool these days) with the absolute confidence that not a single person doubts the fact that I am extremely well off. I would not even have to wonder about whether or not people were aware of the fact that all my fashion choices were purchased with tons of money, so it's all good.

When brown people dress poorly, they must be poor. When white people dress to look poor, they end up on the runway. I'll have me a piece of that polyester pie, please.

### I would correct everyone's pronunciation
Do you know how many white people have corrected my pro-nunciation? Most of them have been journalists, which makes this next point even worse, because in conversation with those same people I have been asked to use simple English they can understand. And it's not because my English is bad. It's because it's better than theirs and they don't know 'big' words.

If I were white, I would spend an entire day correcting every-one's pronunciation of the word 'croissant' without ever bothering to learn how to use or even speak words like 'discourse', 'appre-hensive' or 'ostentatious'. At the same time, I would expect, nay, *demand* that everyone I interact with understand and speak the language of my people without ever making any effort to do the same for them.

### I would name my kids after an animal or a fruit
Whites have a lot to say about the names of people from other cultures. They cannot get rid of this bad habit. It started ages ago

41

and stuck to them like the smallpox they handed out with the blankets they swapped for land back in colonial times. Thing is, they didn't only take the land, they took the people from the land as well. What they forgot to take, however, were those people's names. And then they gave them new ones.

So in South Africa we have a whole bunch of months walking around. The September families, the October families, the Tituses – yeah, that's right, when they ran out of months, they started calling people by the names of the ships they dragged them here on. What's in a name? A slave by any other name would work as hard, right?

White people can't 'name-call' any more, but their past has ruined them because now, when they have to learn people's actual names, they can't do it. Their tongues abandon them faster than the forefathers who left them here.

I went through most of my schooling being referred to as Haaa-yeee Dow-yeee. The Mohamed bit in the middle was ignored. I think it's because the teachers weren't quite sure how to mess that part up. Anyway, Haaa-yee Dow-yee I was. Is it Arabic, is it Egyptian, is it Indian? The answers did not matter; it was not regarded as South African, so it wasn't really a name.

But white people, white people can be anything they want to be. So much so that now that they have run out of names for themselves, they can even be Apples, Pears or Jackfruits.

If you can name your kid anything without anyone batting an eye, why not push the now slaveless boat out a little more?

If I were white I would name my kid after some weird rare animal. Like Tasseled Wobbegong, for example. Or Wunderpus Photogenicus. I can see myself standing at the school gate, dressed in my boho-chic run-around clothes, chatting to the mom of Haaa-yee Dow-yee and saying, 'Gosh. Your kid's name is so hard to say … Oh. Sorry. Here comes my son Wunderpus Photogenicus. Gotta go.' Now wouldn't that be a Wunderpus thing?

**I would save money on spices and spend money on a gap year**
Guys. The elusive gap year is the slap that keeps on giving. White people are the sole beneficiaries of the gap year. The gap year is to white people what cheese is to pizza. They just go together. And when they go, they go to London to au pair, or to Australia to help farm aborigines or aubergines or whatever (who knows what they get up to down there) and, obviously, they check out emigration prospects. They also do things like go to the US to assist kids of a First World nation at summer camp, or they go to Alaska to ski for a couple of months of the year and work in a resort for the rest. Meanwhile the rest of us are back here grafting because our parents don't have money or time for nonsense.

Then one day, we all meet on the playing field that is the professional environment and we're talking about that time we worked in the back kitchen at a Juicy Lucy and the first five pages of Brittany's CV has a list of international 'job' experiences. Let's get real here: a gap year is 365 days of doing as little as possible with as much funding from your parents as possible. White people are so privileged, they can afford to go and do nothing for a year *and* come back to have a tertiary education.

I have figured out why. The answer, my friends, is in the spices. White people don't spend any money on spices, ever. Spices are offensive to white people. They once stole them from a wide variety of countries, and now they refuse to use them so they will not pay for them.

The spice market is doing well in South Africa because the majority of our population have taste. But it's the minority who have money. And they will not throw it away on spices. Well, I am happy to throw some spice here: I would love to be white for just one day so that my mouth would be happy with the taste of food as bland as sawdust, in exchange for a lovely year or two overseas for niks.

### I would make a hobby of going to property viewings

Making an appointment to view a property you would like to rent as a person of colour is hard. I cannot count the number of times I have had a white friend call an agent for me (if the agent was white as well) *just* so that I could get in. Making an appointment to view a property you would like to *buy* as a person of colour is even worse. Like the time I bought a flat and the agent who was sent to meet me and who had her German ancestry on full display – I could tell from her socks and sandals – looked me up and down and literally questioned if I was sure *I* was able to afford the flat. Obviously I smiled and said yes. Inside I burnt with the desire to say something like: 'Are you sure you can afford to abuse everyone's eyes with that foot fashion you're trying to work?' But I didn't. See? Suffocation.

Anyway, she further interrogated whether I would be able to get a bond, etc. When I told her I could pull out my bank statements and show her, she went with another angle. She tried to talk me out of buying the place: 'It's got so many stairs.' 'No one like *you* lives here.' 'It's a very quiet block hey…' (Obviously she assumed that I liked to have a good old phuza Thursday house party.)

A white client pitched up; it was a joint appointment. The agent practically curtseyed when she arrived. During the showing, I was left to wander about by myself; the agent ignored me because she was too busy talking the place up to the white client

44

as though she was about to sell her Nkandla for a millionth of the price. Luckily, her sweetheart colleague walked in. We had a chat, and soon after I went straight to their offices to make my offer. When the racist agent walked in and saw me sign that paper, she made a U-turn and slammed the door behind her. I'm not bothered. I basically own Nkandla now. For a millionth of the price.

The memory of the treatment that white client received has never left me. This agent was ready to lay her own carcass on the floor so that this woman could walk over it to the door of the home only *she* deserved.

If I were white, I would make a hobby out of viewing apartments. Viewing a property would form part of my to-do list. Get vegan cheese. View property. Go to silent disco yoga. Eat vegan cheese. View another property. As a white person, it's all you need to be treated like royalty. Easy-peasy-vegan-cheesy-squeezy.

## I would talk about emigrating. A lot

As a white person, I would have very little to say really. I would have no stories about offensive property agents, no tough decisions to make about whether I should cook a delicious butter chicken or just a plain ol' boiled chicken with maybe some salt. There would be no need to have lengthy after-school conversations with my children about why their names are important and how they need to assert themselves.

As a white person, there would be no need to sit with friends of my own race so I can release the pain of needing to prove how I was worthy of buying a T-shirt earlier that week. I would never return home after work nursing an existential crisis because someone who doesn't know the meaning of the word 'discourse' got their opinions published over and over again to contribute to said discourse (of the country) while my views are constantly overlooked and I have to work twice as hard to get a byline. If I were white, the only thing I would have to talk about is the potential and necessity of eventual emigration. And I would talk about it all the time. I would talk about emigration all the live-long day.

If I were a woke white though – because, you know, I could be – well, then I would fill the gaps between talking about emigration with healthy servings of crushing guilt about the past. That would make me feel like dying. Then, to recover, I would take a time-out at a family farm somewhere in the berg where I could escape the realities of the world, cry my woke white tears in secret and find comfort in the utopia I'm certain to discover once I emigrate anyway.

Those are all the things I would do if I were white. But do I really want to be white?

This list probably seems like a shallow rant of trivialities, but the difference between being able to do these things freely and without consequence and not being able to do them at all is the difference between a human being who shouts proudly and a human being who walks through the world holding their breath. Forever aware of the fact that, at any given moment, they may have to use that harboured oxygen to explain or defend themselves.

When you are white, you are born in full bloom. It takes little effort to grow into yourself, into who you are, because the seeds of your identity were sown for you a very long time ago. Being white is simple. Being a person of colour is anything but. Being a person of colour is confusing.

It's a rollercoaster of searching and finding. Being a person of colour is hostility. It's pessimism and pride all at once. Being a person of colour is manic depression. Being a person of colour is change.

No textbook offers us the guidelines for this journey. The changes in ourselves happen so quickly sometimes that we don't even recognise them. We have no choice but to change. And that's okay, because change is good. Changing ourselves means that the silent days filled with adversity can become the triumphant days of knowing exactly what to say. But change doesn't happen all at once. And in between there are periods of waiting. They seem long. Sometimes waiting feels like the only thing we've ever done. Waiting our turn. Waiting for the right moment to react. Waiting to find the right words to say. Waiting to feel entitled and privileged. Waiting to feel... superior.

But the truth is I would rather wait than go around begging to be white. Because while I am waiting, I am growing, and while I am growing, I am preparing. I am preparing to take those fierce and tender breaths as I move through a world that suffocated itself because it insisted on staying the same.

# And how the women
# of Islam did slay

If Bibi Aisha (second wife of the prophet Muhammad) was a *Game of Thrones* character she would be announced thus: Aisha, first of her name, hand of the Prophet, mother of believers, the scholarly and inquisitive, narrator of hadiths, commander of armies, warrior, rider of camels, feminist, lawmaker, lawbreaker, revolutionary. And that's the abridged version.

After the Prophet's death, Aisha led 13 000 soldiers to war in the Battle of the Camel, named after her because she rode a camel. They fought Ali, the Prophet's son-in-law, who had failed to avenge the death of Uth'man, the third Khalifah. The Battle of the Camel is historically considered to be the first civil war of the Islamic world. At its centre, Aisha. Allegedly armed with only a dagger and dressed in loose trousers, a safflower red smock, over-gown and gold jewellery. She lost the battle that day, but she killed a lot of men.

Rumour has it that Islamic extremists like those ISIS creatures are terrified of being killed by women. In 2016, women Kurdish soldiers told the UK's *Telegraph* newspaper that they were the best ISIS deterrents because the creatures would not approach the battlefield when faced by them. Why? Men slayed by women apparently don't get to heaven to claim their seventy-two virgin brides. Because, you know, this is the most important reason to utter the words 'in the name of Allah': He will let you into heaven and reward you with more women to kill, rape, pillage, own and abuse. Good deal.

But if a woman kills you, forget about it. No virgins. The heavenly gates will be closed. Perhaps you will get hell instead, where you will burn in fires of melted brass and human bodies. Having your life taken by such a lowly creature will rob you of your privileges in the afterlife where god rewards morons.

Of course, it's not only Islamic extremists who believe the hogwash of seventy-two virgins acting as personal hoes to men in heaven. Western media has had a field day with this fictional fantasy. In fact, it's the spread of uneducated rumours like these that makes Western media responsible for a vast majority of Islamophobia. We have leftists decrying the anti-feminist narrative of Islam and what they think is in the Quran, and rightists acting out aggressively against 'ludicrous notions' like these alleged Quranic verses. I wish the men on the right would just admit that they're jealous. What patriarchal misogynist doesn't long for seventy-two virgins of their own? Perhaps in another act of kindness, god will satiate their desires with the spirit of jihad.

*I* obviously think the idea of women fighting terrorism and killing men in the field is pretty awesome.

Women in Islam have slayed (with the sword and otherwise) for years. It's a fact. But these facts are secrets. Just don't read the Quran properly, or delve into the research and historical books, okay? Most Muslim people I know don't bother anyway. They're afraid of seeing things they don't want to know. Like how women have lots of rights and are just as entitled to freedoms as men.

But why trade in facts when you can trade in the degradation and exploitation of women? Such fun.

Truth-bomb alert: the Quran is one of the most flexible pieces of text in the history of texts, and it's pretty straightforward about its flexibility. It even spells it out for the reader: 'Some of these verses are definite in meaning and others are ambiguous' (*Sura* 3, v. 7).

A twenty-nine-word sentence in the holy book (for example) has over seventy-two meanings in English. So, basically, people can pick and choose where they want to sow discord. Here's the catch, though: the Quran also makes it clear that only god knows the true meaning of any of the verses. Thus, only god knows which verses are literal and which are not.

I'll tell you what I know, though: you cannot derive meaning from something that does not exist. And there is no mention of the number seventy-two in the Quran. There is no promise that this number will manifest in virgins as a reward to ungovernable men with jihadist tendencies. Plot twist: if this verse (and promise) did exist, then women would be afforded this gift in heaven as well. Because in the Quran, men and women are equal.

The Bible is addressed to men and refers to the second and third person in the masculine. In contrast, the holy book of Islam is the only scripture of the monotheistic religions to address both men and women. It talks of believing men *and* believing women, honourable men *and* honourable women. And again, to make it clear, it talks of their equal standing in life, love, war and everything else. What's good for the guy is good for the gal!

And one of the gals who would receive a whole lot of goodness in heaven because of her killing in the name of Islam is Aisha.

But the idea of getting heavenly rewards for religious killings is fake, like a lot of other preachy beliefs, and only came into being some 300 years after the death of the Prophet. In fact, a lot of Islamic 'laws' pertaining to women only came into being centuries after the revelation of the Quran. Like the obligation to wear hijab, and the restrictions on a woman's right to education and work and ... fun!

But for now, let's ignore the nonsense post-300 years and step back even further. To about 585 CE. Enter Khadija bint Khuwaylid (the Prophet's first wife).

If Khadija, with respect and peace, was a *Game of Thrones* character she would be announced thus: Khadija the great, first of her name, the pure one, the first believer, cornerstone of the Islamic faith, philanthropist, blessed in wealth, businesswoman, proprietor of more caravans than entire Arabian tribes, employer of the Prophet.

Khadija al-Kubra (Khadija the Great) proposed to Muhammad. Yes, she asked *him* to marry her. These were still extremely patriarchal times; they preceded the feminist revolution that followed the solidification of Islam as a formal religion. Khadija's influence is partly responsible for this feminist revolution. Yes, there was feminism. It existed in Islam. In fact, it existed in the Islamic world and was decreed in the Quran long before it existed in the Western world. A lot of the rights afforded to women in the sixth century in the Islamic world were only afforded to women in the Western world in the eighteenth century. Twelve centuries later. That's 1200 years!

Many revelations in the Quran, believe it or not, serve to protect and improve the status of women. These revelations were enshrined in laws at the time. Shariah law today is not what it once was. But let's not trade in facts, remember? Men forbid we ruin the bullshit with truth.

Like how sixth-century laws made the education of girls

a sacred duty and gave women the right to own property. Nowadays, men bury women up to the neck on the property they probably stole from women and stone them. This is a fact.

Pre-Islam, women could not choose whether to marry or not, but Islamic laws state that a woman must always give her consent in order for the marriage to be legitimate. Islam was also the first of the monotheistic religions to give women the right of inheritance and the right to *earn*: 'Men shall have a share of that which they have earned, and women a share of that which they have earned' (*Sura* 4, v. 33).

Khadija was a single mother, a landowner, a wealthy business-woman, the Prophet's boss and, in later years, the only one who believed him when he came to her with the revelation of Islam. I honestly believe that, had it not been for this woman, Islam as we know it today may not have existed. Imagine if instead of saying to him, 'I believe you and I will be a follower,' she said, 'Are you crazy? Stop talking smack and go feed the camels their daily bread.'

Islam rose through Khadija. And her wealth.

As I utter these words, I wait for my fatwa. Bring it.

And while I'm on the subject of fatwa, let me say that that word always reminds me of Salman Rushdie, and Salman Rushdie reminds me of books, and books remind me of libraries, and libraries always remind me of the University of al-Qarawiyyin in Fez (because that's where the oldest library in the world is), and the University of al-Qarawiyyin in Fez always reminds me of Fatima al-Fihri.

If Fatima al-Fihri was a *Game of Thrones* character she would be announced thus: Fatima, first of her name, the curious one, seeker of knowledge, founder of the world's oldest educational institute, founder of the world's first degree-awarding institution.

Fatima was originally from Tunisia, but migrated to Morocco – also an Islamic state, then ruled by King Idris II. Fatima was a young widow when her father died, and because women were allowed to inherit money – fortunes, in fact – and do with it as they pleased, Fatima and her sister Mariam – both exceptionally educated – each founded a university in 859 CE so they could help educate their communities.

Scholars from all over the world visited Al-Qarawiyyin, and Fatima (as well as other women) attended guest lectures well into her old age.

At the time, Al-Qarawiyyin bridged the gap between Islamic studies and Western studies, and it still operates today, making it the oldest educational institute in operation. You know who else operates today? Boko Haram, the Islamic terrorist group responsible for abducting over 200 education-seeking schoolgirls in Nigeria. One small step backwards for already backward men, one giant step back for womankind.

There is a scholarship programme in Fatima's name at Al-Qarawiyyin. It serves to promote intercultural understanding in North Africa. Perhaps those Boko Haram militants should apply.

And those are just a few stories of women in Islam who slayed. There were queens, warriors, artists, Sufi masters, researchers, writers, advisors, political leaders and more.

Today the status of women in Islam has shifted from the front of the class to the back of the mosque, which is literally where women in Islam now stand. From leading wars to being trampled on.

For the most part, women in Islam today exist quietly in the shadows, out of sight and out of mind. I have stopped reading books by Middle Eastern authors. They make me *naar*. Where are the powerful stories? Where is the #MuslimGirlMagic?

(Yes, I know about Malala. She's cool. But that's not nearly enough.)

This backward thinking when it comes to women's rights is not reserved for hectic Saudis. It's happening in Muslim communities in South Africa as well. Because patriarchy keeps them seen but not heard.

When food is served at Muslim funerals, the men eat first. It's like a scene from a barbaric period drama. The only difference is that the women don't sit in the centre of the floor waiting for bones to be thrown at them. They get to hang about elsewhere. But within earshot of the men's requests. So in between feasting and talking, the male folk can be easily catered to.

Here's another example. At Muslim weddings (and in general), women have to dress modestly to avoid the male gaze. This is of course over and above the fact that in some really conservative cases the women are separated from the men by a large, thick curtain. We must not tempt these gods with our satanic presence. We must not 'ask' for it. Then, of course, there is the religiously liberal reason for all of this: men are weak, they can't help it, it is a woman's responsibility to help them be decent human beings who can keep it in their pants. I am unavailable for this nonsense, thank you very much. Help yourself or go away.

There are no women who lead the prayers, or deliver the sermons and the speeches. There are no Muslim women who oversee marriages and bless unions. Not that I know of, and not that I have seen. And I have been to a lot of Muslim weddings. In Indian Muslim communities, girls tend to get married as early as sixteen because this is mostly the only goal they're allowed in life. A lot of them aren't *victims*; they're pretty enthusiastic about this life of theirs. But I believe firmly in the words of Maya Angelou: 'When you know better, you do better.' And how can women know better when female scholars who receive airtime in Muslim communities are so few and far between?

More than that, when's the last time Muslim men – youths or elders – attended a talk or religious gathering led by a woman? How many male Muslim feminists are there? I will eat my hat if you can point out more than five in a community I have a relationship with. Like Laudium.

All of this results in a male-directed narrative. It results in men talking to men about what men have to say about men in the Muslim community. More than that, it means men get to talk to men about what men think about women and their place in society. It's like a cult. Honestly. And this cult of modern-day Islam has made me extremely anti-religious.

Aisha never stood for this kind of shit. Why should I?

I'll go to mosque when I can stand at the front.

I offer you this piece of information from the International Association of Sufism (this knowledge is presented because of my inherent Islamic duty and my inherent Islamic guilt, but also because Sufism is something I can get behind):

Islam is a religion where your temple is not a building but your heart; your preacher is not a priest but your intellect; and if your religion is founded upon mere imitation, you are a blasphemer.

In Islam, ignorance is an unforgivable sin, so is your evasion of responsibility for yourself as well as towards all the members of the living world, past and present.

It is incorrect to blame Islam for the shortcomings of its followers, which are the failings of most of humankind.

A religion that is centred on the rights of human beings, and sets both men and women free from the chains of bondage, should not be used in propaganda for the sake of condemnation.

So if you must practise, go with god, not with men.

# Bar brawl with my brother

My brother visited me in Sea Point for the first time in a year. He's six years younger than I am and super cool. I wanted to give him a good time and be cool too. Rebecca and I took him to dinner in Bree Street, very hip, and then we wandered down Shortmarket Street and found ourselves at Manila Bar for karaoke. He fell asleep on the couch while a couple of students belted out Bon Jovi. He's a good-looking kid: I got the Jet store genes, he got the designer set. So even while he was catching a few winks on a dirty, torn pleather couch, a young woman and her friends proceeded to take photos of him. With flash and everything. No shame. Rebecca and I hung out a bit because I wanted to sing, but Justin Bieber did not play, so we left. I didn't want the night to end so I insisted that we stop by Corner Bar, up the road from my place in Sea Point.

Corner Bar is amazing. It's as old as Egypt and disgusting. You can smoke inside and it's tiny. It's always a hot box in there and the patrons are mostly regulars of the male variety. They're middle-aged or older and have the distinct feel about them of either having been kicked out by their partners or just hanging about after a day trawling on the Atlantic. Sometimes, the odd group of youths from the language school next door hangs about. They don't speak much English, so they mostly keep to themselves and don't bug anyone. The older dudes usually don't either, so all things considered, it's fairly comfortable in there for two women who just want to hang out without travelling too far, you know? My brother, always one for atmosphere, was convinced after this sales pitch, so we hopped in and took a booth.

I have never had many physical altercations, except for the odd bullying incident in school, where I was the victim of racism and a tiny moving target who had no friends and was asking for it. I don't think you can really count being pushed down stairs, or having my hair pulled, or even being teased for having a sanitary pad in my blazer pocket after a bunch of mean-girls went through my stuff in the locker room.

If I really stretch my memory, there are two incidents where I fought back. One was in Grade 8, when I was once again being teased. I had had about enough and I ended up using all the fight in me to topple a relatively large boy off his chair because he was talking smack about my mom. Then there was this one time during lunch break when I was at the centre of an actual 'barney' with my sister's nemesis. I was defending my sibling's honour this time. I can't remember what against. I do remember the cigarette I had under the tree at the lapa afterwards with the other losers who only spoke to each other to borrow lighters. It was fantastic. Stuyvesant Red. The loose draw, the painter's cigarette, disgusting and totally worth it.

I got a bleeding mouth when I was shoved in primary school, but garnered no other physical scars from these episodes. But that's okay; I am a gold medallist at falling over my own feet, so I made up for the scars elsewhere. Ankle sprains, fractured wrists, cuts, bruises. Breaking ribs while playing soccer, losing a piece of skin on my elbow during a tennis match (there's still a pruned version of what used to be perfectly healthy epidermis). Your standard knee scrapes, of course. Once, I even dropped a weight on my face at gym.

Seriously, I'm a pro at being clumsy. It's never elegant and it's never heroic. These are not ordinary accidents is what I am getting at. Everyone gets hurt sometimes, but this, this is freak-of-nature stuff. It's almost impossible that one person can be this hopeless at standing on her own two feet. And it's strange, because I have excellent hand–eye coordination. The knack for falling is so bad that when I started longboarding and decided I could get in some good practice by skating to the gym and back, my partner's first words to me when I got home were not 'Hello', but 'Did you fall today?'

Then this Corner Bar brawl happened: my first physical clash as a fully grown human who is still fairly tiny. This drunken white dude from the senior society tripped me with his government-issue crutch. Why would anyone do that to a fragile angel, you ask? Let me tell you.

It was midnight on that Saturday with my brother; the regular crowd had already shuffled in. There was no piano man, but old-school rock classics were playing on the shabby stereo. People were chattier than usual, maybe because it was witching hour. A young white dude, let's call him Dave, walked up to us and cosied up. He started building chats as big as the Carlton Towers, mostly with my brother. He was jolly, from Durban, and that's about all I know. I paid no attention to his conversation, as an introvert who is excellent at zoning out. I needed a break from the white noise so I made my way to the bathroom and, upon exiting, witnessed a kerfuffle.

Dave was storming out, his foreigner friends from the language school trying to restrain him. He was shouting that he didn't want to be there any more. He didn't want to be with 'this racist'. The restraining attempt ended up outside. I'm not one to miss out on observational treats, so I followed, but it was boring. I went back in to take my seat and discovered that Dave's rant about 'this racist' was in reference to the crutch-bearing geriatric I mentioned previously. Let's call him Asshole.

Before I went to the bathroom, Asshole had hobbled in, foot in cast and smack in mouth. He went straight at me. I was wearing this cap, you see, a really fantastic snapback that I purchased on holiday in Thailand. It says 'Normcore' and I had it on because I was going through my annual bad-hair phase. *'Jou kop is te groot vir daai hoed,'* he said. Then: *'Jou hoed is te groot vir daai kop.'* He couldn't make his mind up; he just wanted a reaction. He was a lonely pain in the ass, I decided. *Soeking*, as we say. I ignored him.

After Dave departed, everyone left in the bar was black except for Asshole, the barman, a young American woman and Rebecca. Asshole became progressively more difficult to ignore. He left my hat alone and proceeded to throw insults at us about our race while sipping on his Windhoek Lager. We started off passive. 'Just finish your beer and go home, man,' my brother said. I chuckled a bit on the inside. The ignorance of this old human was kind of hilarious, but also dangerous. Consider the amount of privilege and self-confidence he had to have to throw this crap around in a bar full of young people of colour where he was clearly outnumbered.

When he started having a go at my brother, I felt the heat rise in my throat. I was about to spit fire.

'You go home,' Asshole sneered. 'I live in a place you people can't even afford. I will call the apartheid police for you. Verwoerd would have known what to do with you people. He would have thrown you to the dogs. You guys are dogs!'

I turned on him. 'Call them! Call the apartheid police, man!' Lame, I know. But trust me, it's hard to insult a white man with an inflated sense of self who is so … average. Below average.

'I am a dog! I am a dog!' my brother shouted. 'Want to see?' And he proceeded to howl. Next-level stuff.

This guy was the barman's friend, so the barman got involved. To his credit, he asked Asshole to settle down, told him what he was saying wasn't allowed and then asked us to settle down as well. At this point the American woman chirped in: 'Come on guys, can't we all just get along?' I could not contain my rage: again, a misplaced sense of involvement and entitlement. How dare she? No one asked her. She needed to find a lane.

'Shut the fuck up or leave,' I said. I am not proud of this profanity. Rebecca promptly left the scene to stand outside. Armed with a healthy inquisitiveness, however, she peered in through the window every so often, and had her phone in her hand. I think she was ready to call Netcare or something.

The barman called a rent-a-cop: a general security dude in the area. He strolled in, tall and thick, a coloured bloke with a very Spanish name.

'Here's the apartheid police. Throw them out, throw them out,' yelled Asshole, swinging his crutch. The barman also requested that we please leave. Were these people serious? I went up to the Spanish-named rent-a-cop and explained the racist ranter's offences. We all shouted and made it very clear that we were not going to be thrown out unless he was thrown out first. What typical politically incorrect crap was this? As people of colour *we* had to leave? Nah. It was not flying. The African students agreed and stuck to their seats. The American subsided, mostly out of fear. Rebecca monitored her phone's battery out-side. The Human Rights Commission should have an emergency number, in my personal opinion. Mr Security Man was relatively understanding and gently nudged Asshole out of the bar. Ass-hole took a seat at the picnic table outside and waited for us with crutch bated. As soon as he left, we peacefully exited, the bar empty, the barman locking doors. No more classic rock.

Still convinced that he had achieved gold-medal status in the race Olympics, Asshole carried on ranting that we had experienced the power of whiteness and the apartheid police. My brother walked up to him and spat at his feet. It was the most reactive and aggressive I have ever seen him. Aside from the random grunt and fist in the air because he gets frustrated when designing inner-city buildings, he is a totally laid-back guy. I was a bit proud of him, to be honest.

'I'll fuck you up! I'll fuck you up!' Asshole shouted, swinging his crutch and aiming for my brother as best he could despite his early-onset dementia and clear inebriation.

I lost my cool. 'Fuck him up, fuck him up!' I raged, and went straight for him. The students held me back. And as they released me, Asshole tripped me with his crutch. I fell face-first and broke my fall with the palm of my hand. I now have a scar on my right hand that is not the result of my own clumsiness, but proof of an aggressive racial attack.

We left, Rebecca relieved and strung out. The African stu-dents chased after us; they wanted to hang out. Misery loves company and all that, or strength in numbers? 'Absolutely not. We are going home,' said Rebecca. And so we did.

At home, I lay on my balcony looking at the stars to calm down. I saw Orion. Fixed as it was and always has been, I came to the conclusion that this was the disposition of the racist South

African white male. Stuck and armed with a metaphorical sword (or crutch). Rebecca appeared and asked me if all that commotion was really necessary. This did not help my fury. She went to bed. I was dumbstruck by her question.

She later explained that she was worried that the incident would play out with the standard narrative if it escalated any further. The headline would read: 'Black hoodlums attack crippled pensioner'. Fair point. In the moment, I had not considered this.

Honestly though, as a person of colour in a situation like that, you reach the point where you accept that even if it's a skewed headline you get, that's the prize. Getting angry and saying something is worth it. Being the bigger person is exhausting and sometimes it's just bullshit.

We've been to Corner Bar since. The Caucasian barman did not recognise the 'black hoodlums'. It was a peaceful experience. Not all whites, I guess.

# Zwelenzima Vavi and Helen Zille are starting a super party

The first time I met Basil I didn't really meet him at all. It was more like I imagined him. It was my first night in an apartment in Gardens after finishing my honours in journalism at Stellenbosch University. I had no furniture so I slept on the floor in the open-plan lounge on the deflated carcass of a blow-up mattress. I was uncomfortable, I was anxious, and when the Gandalf-like silhouette appeared at my kitchen window, I was scared.

I was prepared to suffer on the floor for a couple of days, inhaling the sand and dust the wind swept in, but nothing could have prepared me for this vision. It was so weird that I convinced myself that the exhaustion of the move had made me delirious. I wanted a sleeping pill more than anything. The howling south-easter whipped Basil's hair about, and because he was only a shadow, I couldn't tell if he was facing out or looking in. Had he been staring at me through the frosted window for the longest time, or was he trying his best to be blown off the harbour-facing balcony of the fourth floor?

After actually making his acquaintance days later, I discovered Basil's love for chats. He always managed to catch me on my way up to my apartment after a long day at *YOU* magazine. As entertaining as he was, I couldn't call his lengthy anecdotes welcome at that time of the day. I appreciated them more in memory. He seemed to spend less time in his apartment than he did wandering the corridors, chain-smoking cheap cigarettes. The silhouette made sense once I had a grasp of his walkabout tendencies. He smoked on that balcony with his wizard hair blowing in the wind every night. If my apartment looked like his, I probably would have done the same. I managed to peek inside one night while waiting for the elevator. It looked like a storeroom, the passageway crowded with buckets and tins and old scraps of tile. You could see right into the lounge, which was just as cluttered. The centrepiece of the room was an old IBM computer, circa 1990. Not an antique, but a trusty piece of equipment I would hear more about later. The apartment was completely dark but for a dim red light giving the place the feel of a *kamer* in Amsterdam.

If I didn't know any better, I'd say that Basil was lonely and hunting for human interaction. He would watch the alleys and as soon as you took the corner, he would pounce and launch straight into some narrative. But Basil was happy to be alone. Not lonely, just alone.

One afternoon when I was home early, he leant between the bars of my gate because the door was open and started to tell me a bit about his life. He was married once, he had two kids and he used to be a drug addict. 'I'm not any more,' he said. 'I got rid of my wife and, thank god, I don't see my kids any more.' If this family stuff had come from anyone else, it would have seemed bitter and sad. But Basil really sounded like he was relieved to be done with all of it.

The 'I was a druggie' bit helped piece together the puzzle of his appearance. Thin, although not frail for his age. Pale, papery skin marked with the odd homemade tattoo turning blue because of cheap ink and sunlight. Long, white, wizard tresses, of course. Basil wasn't tall; you got the sense life had whittled him down quite a bit. But even though time had eroded his physique, it seemed to have done the opposite for his mind and imagination. Basil didn't chat out of desperation for company; he talked because he was a storyteller.

One of the most important ingredients in storytelling is memory, because good storytelling is a lot like cooking a signature dish. You have to remember how to do it the same way again and again and again. If you do, the senses tingle and you smile with pride. It sends a ping to your heart, sometimes a sense of nostalgia and, every so often, a degree of self-worth. By adding some of your own secret spice, you can make any narrative gastronomic. Sometimes, your memory of how to make your signature meal, how to string the story together, fails. When that happens, you take the remains and try to concoct something new and delicious.

The second most important ingredient of storytelling is emotion. Your muscles have to move with what you're saying. As the storyteller, though, you have to try your best to remain detached because the tale no longer belongs to you once you've served it. Word for word, it exits you and enters someone else. The audience must want the story more than you do. The point of telling it, after all, is that you hope they will make more of it. You want it to make them feel something real, something sincere and organic, whether it's bitterness or beauty, anger or awe, sadness or soulfulness. It can be one of these things or it can be all. And so you must peel yourself away from your own words and feelings, and accept that your meaning is going to turn into someone else's. When you tell a story, you teach someone something about yourself. More than that, what any good storyteller can hope for is that their story will teach the listener or reader something about themselves.

When you're confident of both these ingredients, you put your chef's hat on and show people what you can do. Sometimes, the results are bad. Maybe you ruined the dish. But that's the risk any storyteller takes. It's a gamble Basil was willing to take over and over again.

'I'm writing a book about Russian Jews in South Africa,' he told me once. 'I've been working on it for the past twenty years. I have a computer: that's where I write.' He was wearing his favourite pink Puma T-shirt. It was a youth size so it fitted like a crop top. He paired this with synthetic white clam-diggers and the worn Hi-Tec sandals that he donned on his walks to Camps Bay and back. He invited me to join him for this lengthy stroll one Saturday morning. I politely declined. It was sweet of him, but I didn't have a pair of trusty hiking sandals, and it was too long a walk for my liking.

By my estimation, Basil was at least seventy-something, which meant he'd started banging away at that old IBM when he was fifty years old or so. All his recollections and research into Cape Town's history of the Russian Jews were safely tucked away in that dusty computer's hard drive. No USB port, no backup. The only way to save something externally? A floppy disk. Those thin, black, square plastic diskettes, called floppies because they could literally bend in half, rendering them useless. So I assumed that Basil would never get rid of the dinosaur computer because there was no way, in this day and age, that he would find floppies to save stuff on. But on an elevator ride up with my brother one night, a Sherlock Holmes–looking uncle wearing a coat and a hounds-tooth hat joined us. He supported himself with a walking stick in one hand and in the other he carried a bunch of these archaic record-keeping 'albums'. He was Basil's friend and he was on his way to help back up the big book.

I don't know how much one could write on the history of the Russian-Jewish people in Cape Town. Before Basil, I had no idea it was even a 'movement'. I'd assumed that it was such a tiny book that a few floppies would suffice and that Basil was exaggerating when he said, over and over again, that he had already penned at least 20 000 pages and he was far from done. Basil was a good storyteller, but I always got the impression that he only spoke the language of illusion. I ate the fantasies he created without a knife or fork so that I could taste them with my own two hands, but a book on the Russian Jews of Cape Town that would turn out to be longer than five volumes of *War and Peace*? I still don't think I could ever feast on that. I Googled the topic a couple of years later; Russia does not show up once in the entire Wikipedia entry of the history of Jewish people in South Africa. The Jewish genealogy database doesn't throw out any information either.

Another one of Basil's favourite topics was South African politics post 1994. 'The ANC Youth League have disbanded because Zille and Vavi are scooping all of them up to have more power,' he once said. 'You see all that empty coastline?' He pointed to the horizon from the balcony. 'They're going to fill that up with low-cost housing, overpopulate it and take over the country. They want to overthrow the government. Helen Zille and Zwelenzima Vavi are starting a super party. Just watch. I'm not a racist, but you can say goodbye to the Western Cape as you know it now.'

How to engage with something like this? Unclear.

What was clear at this stage, though, was that Basil traded

fairy tale as fact and dragged the listener into moments of belief or disbelief so powerful that the facts mattered less than the story itself because he told them so well. He got the storytelling recipe right, again and again and again.

I still know nothing about the great Russian-Jewish exodus to South Africa. I do know I want to tell stories like Basil did. I want to lead the listener and, before I have taken them too far, or lost them forever, I want to leave them with stories of their own. I'll trade facts instead of fairy tales, but I will definitely add some of my own secret spice.

# A resignation letter
# to performative whites

Dear performative whites

Please accept this as my letter of resignation.

In the last few years I have been flooded with emotions when it comes to you. So much so that I could not focus on them. It has been an abusive relationship. There is a scientific term for it: Stockholm Syndrome.

This is difficult for me to admit. Embarrassing, even, but I have worked hard to find the courage to openly say this to you: I have allowed you to hold me captive for far too long. Your virtue signalling and performative wokeness have led me to try to make myself believe that I have some sort of psychological alliance with you. I have, on several occasions, tricked myself into having affection and trust for you. For far too long, I have struggled to reconcile these misplaced feelings with my true opinions about you. The very opinions I kept silent out of fear of you and a desperate need for you to like me more. I was trying to feel accepted.

*We're not all mean and out to get you. We're not all that bad. Some of us are here to appreciate and help you. We recognise your efforts and we are grateful.* These were words of inspiration I often uttered in my mind, and even out loud. I used them to drive myself further into your minds and your hearts. I used them as weapons to fight my way through the dark motherboard of your whiteness. I used them as a shield to defend your white fragility. I did not realise I was only using them to defend myself.

You see, for a long time I thought that making excuses for your inability to admit to ignorance (because you were so busy being better than the rest of your kind) sometimes made me feel like a better human being. But it did not make *me* feel like a better person at all. It only made *you* feel that I was a better person. That I was better than all the other people of colour. Passive. Nothing to be scared of here. And this is disturbing. This is exactly the same behaviour that open racists ask of people like me.

Well, I have had enough.

Perhaps my 'loyalty' towards your cause, my support for your willingness to lead the marches and write the op-eds, my eagerness to share your Facebook status updates, has made me feel lucky. Lucky, because I tricked myself into believing that you were charming little snowflakes in a sky tormented by dark clouds raining vitriol. But really, what you were doing was colonising the struggle. Our struggle.

You set up your tents of privilege on ground we fought hard to stand on. And we are only beginning. But your inability to recognise the wrongness of your actions leaves little room for us to develop. And so we have started to bravely approach the frontlines with our words, our thoughts. We will fight you for our space because we can.

Previously, I would have educated you with carefully chosen words because I did not want to be the painful cause of your white tears. But I am hydrated now. Your white tears have 'nourished' me. I cannot drink from your fountain of self-induced sympathy any longer. I do not feel sorry for you. Going to pro-tests and painting underprivileged schools in underprivileged areas does not remove your whiteness. And it does not remove our pain. You will not colonise our pain. You have no right to it. It is not yours, nor is this fight.

I cannot express in words how much your monopoly over the media makes me burn with agony. Your righteousness makes headlines, your wokeness occupies way too much space in news-papers and websites, and your virtue signalling at the forefront of any one of *our* fights makes me want to go blind so that I do not have to see you. What hurts the most is your inability to recognise how all of this is effectively working against any good intentions you might have. You often cannot admit to and face the role that your white privilege plays in all of this.

It sounds as though I am a silent observer harbouring an inherent anger towards white skin, regardless of the person who occupies it. That my words are the result of a gene that exists purely to hate you. That is not the case. I am the product of much personal experience with your kind. The good whites (those so tainted by their own moral superiority complex that they are unable to see the error of their ways) and the bad (those who openly wear their hatred on their sleeves).

My preference, for the record, is for the latter. Give me an open racist any day. At least they wear their ignorance with con-viction. They do not demand an education and they are not exhausting to me. They are, in some ways, okay with their power-lessness. And their openness about their beliefs, however ill, makes me feel driven and empowered. They cannot take anything from me, and they do not try. If they do, I do not have to bother treating them with the same tender care woke whites demand. You drive me a bit mad. I have felt insane for long enough.

I do not appreciate your whitesplaining. I do not appreciate your armchair liberalism. I will no longer stand for the fact that you will speak on behalf of me, and take such great measures to separate yourself from your own kind because you think you are better. I no longer have time for that. I am entitled to my opinion. Listen, or walk away.

Your virtue signalling extends beyond the privilege of having a voice that shouts louder. You are parading your convictions. You think they separate you from your own communities and you try desperately to do so. However, your need to appear virtuous only distracts you, and you alone, from the fact that you are merely letting people know how good you are. You are asking us to believe in your goodness. Doing so makes you feel like a better person too.

We see through it. I have personally learnt to clear my mind of 'appreciation' for you. Your virtue signalling is a humblebrag. It is a way to camouflage your vanity and self-aggrandisement. You make statements and act out in 'charitable' ways to garner approval. You reach for this approval through Twitter and Instagram. Your photos with black children, your visits to the outskirts of town, are all for vanity, and this vanity is worse than any other kind because you drape it in selfless conviction. Is it selfless if it serves you so much? What's more, you are less concerned with how much it serves you in the eyes of people of colour. Yes, you want to 'stand out' with us, but really, your virtue signalling is designed to present yourself as 'woke' among other white people. It's ammo. It is a shallow, lazy way to rebut arguments and prove that you are better than the rest without actually educating yourself on how not to act like an authority on the issues of race relations and inequality. You are not cool. This is not cool. It is not clever either.

I know you are not perfect. I'm not resigning because of your imperfections. I am not perfect either. And before you ask me to qualify these things for you again, let me do it one last time: yes, you are or can be a good person. I know that you did not ask to be born white and I get that you try to not be racist and make efforts to avoid contributing to racist agendas. But understand that you still belong to an institution of privilege. An institution built on discrimination and racism. An institution that still benefits you in all the ways I mentioned above, and more.

How many times have you been followed around in a store? How many times have customers in an upmarket grocery store looked you up and down because they think you should be shopping somewhere else? How many times have you been asked to leave a place because of a white person who should have been asked to leave instead? How many times has a white person in a store come up to you and mistaken you for an employee? In an airport lounge recently, my friend Sarah was asked by an old white woman to 'bring more cups'. This has never happened to any of my white friends.

How many times have you been called a terrorist? How many times has some failure of yours been cause to judge your entire race? How many times have you felt insecure in a public space because your skin was too dark? How many times have you been denied access to something? Anything? How many times has an estate agent questioned your income when you went to rent or purchase an apartment even though you came with receipts? Or just not got back to you? Zero.

Just because you consider yourself a woke white does not make you immune to the advantages society offers you. Admitting this is painful for you because you think you're so different. But I do not care about that pain any longer. It is time to admit to it and educate yourself on it. Instead of virtue signalling, start getting real.

Start getting real about the fact that you have a lot to learn when it comes to noticing and acknowledging the privilege you have. I have had these conversations with you one too many times. You do not rise above your privilege because you consider yourself better. If you were better, my calling you out would not offend you. And I would not feel the need to tread carefully around you because you are sensitive and fragile. Think about it. I should not have to walk on eggshells around you and your efforts.

In conversation, I have so often been confronted by woke whites who are quick to use their privilege when it suits them simply because the option is available. When confronted with topics of race and discrimination and the inevitable role they play in all of it, regardless of whether they are openly racist or not, they often resort to victim-blaming. It goes something like this:

'How do you expect us to help if you won't change?'

'How do you expect me to learn if you won't respect my sensitive nature and pain?'

And then, of course, there is the stock response of 'not all white people'. This is, in itself, a statement of power. You are part of the problem that perpetuates oppression when you say this. It is a way of walking away from accountability. Your privilege has been called out and it hurts you so you exert your superiority to escape the conversation. You feel entitled to do that. To not talk about it when you don't want to. And you can pick your battles, usually according to one key factor: Will the battle make you feel like a better person? Will it serve your sense of self and inspire an Oscar-worthy performance of wokeness? Answer yes, and there you are. Present. Practising. Performing.

I once thanked you for your participation. And participated along with you. I once accepted the role of trainer, helper and scriptwriter even. But your personal and selective disengagement from your own privilege only says one thing to me: my ongoing struggle does not matter to you. So now you must coach yourselves.

Dear performative whites, I cannot separate my thoughts from how the world operates. I cannot leave the direct and negative implications of that world behind. I do not have the luxury or the privilege of extricating myself from it. I cannot afford that. I have no virtue to signal to *you* any more. I can no longer afford your voice and actions and humblebrags at the cost of my own silence. I will no longer pay for your journey with my pain.

I quit. With immediate effect.

Wishing you well on this journey you must take alone.

Sincerely,
HAJI MOHAMED DAWJEE

# Depression: A journal

**Age 6**

I hate being apart from my parents, yet I feel separated from them all the time. I feel invisible. When they go, I am afraid that they will not come back. I have learnt to watch the moon for safety. It anchors me and lets me know I am real and I exist. It gives me company and helps me believe they will return for me. I don't mind feeling unseen in their presence, as long as I know they are there.

I am six years old and the anxiety of separation has not left me. I try to test myself and be brave. I hope that doing things like going for sleepovers at my cousin's place will help me understand that separation is only temporary. I convince myself I can have a good time before things return to my normal. It never works. I have spent so many nights weeping. Keeping aunts awake. My insides unstable with fear like a ship caught in a storm with no end in sight. I feel like I will die and I wait for the day. The nights always feel long and lonely and endless. I do not know the smells. I do not know the sounds. They are strangers to me and they make me feel stranger.

## Age 8

My sister joins me on sleepovers now. It's nice. I get to take something I know with me. I enjoy the safety net she provides without even knowing that she does. She is younger than me so I pretend to be her guardian when actually she is mine.

My cousin, sister and I have endless roles to play in our world of adventure. We get lost in fiction. As time goes by and bedtime nears, the same weight of worry seeps into me. Things are about to change and I am about to feel terrible. It becomes harder to get lost in child's play. I take a step back and as I exhale to compose myself I observe the confidence of my sibling. She is unperturbed. Unbothered. Consumed by fun. I try to take a page out of her book, but the fact that I am pretending is too real to me.

Dinner arrives. We are fed. Then it's bath time. Then we all gather in front of the TV to watch whatever the grown-ups are watching as long as it is suitable. My mind is working. The whole time. I am a robot, ready for regular programming to resume. My wiring will fuse soon and I will lie in bed and stare at the ceiling consumed by discomfort and distress. I will do all of this in silence because I do not want to embarrass myself. I am the oldest and so I am supposed to be the bravest.

## Age 9

There is an argument going on. I can hear the muffled reverberations of conflict sweep through the floor of our tiny house. It keeps me awake, and it makes my body coil. I am frozen with fear. But I share a bedroom with my brother and sister. If I can hear it, they can hear it too. I feel responsible for them. If my nerves need calming, theirs do too. I lift my head from under the duvet. My brother is fast asleep. Sleep is so easy for a three-year-old. I like that his world is made of dreams. My sister is awake. I distract her with duvet forts. I know, in my heart, that I want to distract myself as well.

## Age 11

I can't seem to shake this feeling of hate I have for myself. I wander through the house feeling lost. I leave my graffiti everywhere. I scratch 'I hate myself' on old bits of polystyrene that I know will soon be discarded, and I carve the same stamp on the insides of cupboards where I know no one will find them. If it is found, I will be reprimanded for ruining the furniture. Sometimes, I am brave enough to etch my message on a doorframe or wall. I do it subtly, but it is there. In my heart I hope someone will see it and save me. I hope I will be saved from feeling imperfect and someone will teach me to love myself more. But I know it won't happen. I have started to think of death. I start to think of suicide. I think of it often now. I want to leave my body, but I don't want to go anywhere. I have no idea how to do that, how to escape myself. I have resorted to living with self-hatred instead.

## Age 14

High school sucks. Everyone belongs somewhere. I don't. Friends are few, and I pretend to be part of a group even though I don't quite fit in. Everyone seems to have a group. Everyone has a clique to rally with and go to the mall with. There's the sports group and the arty group and the academic group, and everyone is cool.

I have started smoking. There is a group of students who don't really belong to anyone, and they sit under the tree at the tennis courts and sneakily puff away. The Blazer Brigade. They don't even belong to each other, but they're loyal. Someone always has a cigarette and someone always has a lighter. Nothing else matters. I wish I could sit there all the time instead of going to class.

The problems in class continue. I can't concentrate, I hardly find anything interesting and everyone knows I am a loser. I wish I did not have to do this. I suck at it and my report cards suck too. I am always scared to take them home, where I remain a failure and a deserving target of disciplining and frustration. My siblings swim in the A-stream while I drown in an eternal pool of disappointment and discontent.

## Age 17

I am in matric. I am so happy this high-school thing is all finally over, although now I wish it would continue, on a loop. Nothing is scarier to me than the reveal of my marks. Their immeasurable potential for further disappointment. Those little percentages in black and white. Failure confirmed by the government.

I pretended to study really hard, but I hid more interesting books between the pages of my textbooks. I have swapped electives more times than I can count. Technical drawing, computer science, art, business economics. I can't believe I finished my last year with business economics. What was I thinking? I knew all the things, but I didn't know all the things, if you know what I mean? The teachers talk at us. I don't know how to listen to that. Things settle in my brain long enough for a pass mark though, without having to recite notes like a parrot. Something I am hopeless at anyway. What's the point of trying?

I am waiting for my university exemption with a tummy tied in knots. If these knots unravel, I will have nothing left to hold on to. They are my curse and cure, all at once. I am in Cape Town on holiday and we are staying with family. I am supposed to SMS my exam number to a mobile hotline at midnight to receive my results.

I need a cigarette, but there is nowhere to smoke. I am imprisoned by the house and my thoughts. I forget about smoking. Getting my marks and getting caught smoking on the same day would be way too much for me to bear. The thought of being caught out in front of an extended family makes me cringe with pre-emptive embarrassment. I wait for the response from the hotline while acting confident and hanging out with cousins. It comes through. An exemption. There is a family lunch the next day. A celebration with apprehension. I feel a weird mixture of achievement and self-deprecation. Next stop: university.

## Age 18

The head of the law department at the University of Pretoria has basically kicked me out. On an emotional level, I feel as though my family has kicked me out too, especially my dad, whom I have disappointed academically.

I wrote the exams that interested me. English and psychology. The law papers had my student number and name scrawled across the top. Nothing else. No questions answered, nothing. I do not want to be a lawyer, but my academic options were spelled out for me by my high-achieving family: dentist (too stupid), doctor (too stupid) or lawyer (inevitably too stupid). And here I am.

I spend my days at home now, under strict supervision. I am not allowed to be left alone. Even my younger brother and sister are regarded as chaperones. I feel more lost and insignificant than ever before. I was caught smoking not long ago. The consequences were rough. I had no mode of defence. Backchats are not allowed.

I have no money on me, ever. It has all been taken away. I have no access to my bank account even though the money in there has been saved from odd jobs like packing groceries at the supermarket. I can't physically go to the bank and get it because I am not allowed out the house on my own. I can only accompany others while they run their own errands.

I spend my days working with my dad at his practice. I do his accounts and load his data and the 'before and after' pictures of his patients on to the computer. When the admin is done, I help him out as his dental assistant. I watch him band braces on teenagers and wait to pass him probes. I lose myself in depression and hopelessness, and this makes me deaf to his requests sometimes. I get angry with myself for being so bad at this simple, easy job.

I have no way to communicate with anyone. No cellphone. No friends. No social life. I read. A lot.

I steal the odd painkiller from the medicine cupboard to self-soothe. It's never enough to keep me asleep forever, but I always carry the hope of that when I go to bed. But then the next day comes and the house is tense. Hardly anyone communicates with me. Their frustration with me has reached saturation point. Understandably. I feel like the plague, something that must be avoided, and then the torturous routine of my day begins again.

## Age 21

I never thought I would be a teacher, but I love it. I started out by teaching second-language English to expat students at the American International School in Pretoria. I was also a full-time aide to Tyler – a kindergarten student with autism who had the tendency to be quite aggressive. Tyler launched into my thigh one day and broke my skin with a bite. Luckily, those days are over. I am now the full-time music teacher.

The kids think I am a high-school senior on account of my height and age; I am the youngest teacher at the school. They are funny and sweet. My life is fuller with them around. And they help my state of mind more than the antidepressants the doctors keep guessing at. Lexamil one week. Depramil the next. I should probably see a specialist. GPs don't seem to be great at this stuff.

Anyway, I can't believe I am actually regarded as a professional in the real world. First I get kicked out of uni. Then I spend six months in a dark hell at home. Then I return to the same university to study music and major in psychology.

Before I returned for that new semester, though, I was given a drug test. My dad drove me to the local clinic. I pissed in a cup and the test came up positive for opiates. I had taken a painkiller that day, but opiates can be anything from codeine to heroin. A strip-search was ordered. My veins were checked. Nothing. I was allowed to go to university.

And a couple of years later, there I was. Certificate in hand and graduate's cap on head. Just before graduation, I got a call from the American school to come in for an interview.

The teaching job pays well and I need the money. It buys me a ticket out of my current life. The job also comes with great medical aid. Which means I can probably see a proper doctor. My dad was so happy when he heard I got a respectable position and I was so happy he felt that way. He actually bought me a car as a gift. A Citi Golf. I love that car. It's much better than the old cheapie I used to drive that needed broomsticks to hold all the windows up.

## Age 22

The high I experienced and the admiration I received from my family for being a teacher did not last long. One night, I was watching an Arsenal–Liverpool match on TV in my bedroom, drifting in and out of sleep. During one of the 'drift in' bits, I heard my dad walk in and huff in disapproval at the TV being on.

I spent the rest of the night with a demon on my chest, counting the hours until morning, when I would face the repercussions.

The repercussions lasted a long time. I was reprimanded for being irresponsible. I was asked to either pay rent so that I could stop freeloading and start being more responsible about things like wasting electricity, or leave. Then I was ignored for a long time so I could think about my options.

The tension and misery hung over the house like an ominous cloud once again and my incompetence, along with my dad's dissatisfaction with me, left everyone unhappy. I am sure they were angry as well. I chose to leave.

I earn enough money to move in with Michelle, a colleague and friend. When she heard what happened at home, she offered me a room in her apartment at a totally affordable price, so I took it.

We get along nicely and it's a lot of fun. I feel a bit better every day and, mostly, I feel like I no longer have to explain my imperfections or compensate for them. My mistakes are just part of who I am. We carpool to work and I have a better social life. For the most part I am happier. The disillusionment sets in every time I visit home. It's a thirty-minute drive to my parents' house, but it feels like three hours there and three hours back. I arrive excited but anxious, because I never know what state I am going to be in when I leave.

## Age 25

Michelle got home and found me on the floor of my bedroom, crying tears of self-hatred and anger. I had visited my parents earlier to watch the French Open. It's a bit of a tradition. It was the men's final. I was joking around with my siblings and at one stage I let out a huge laugh. I was told off about my laughing so I just got up and left. It was a bit more than that, but I won't go into details. I have no idea who won the match that day. I didn't care. I was too sore from being separated from my family one more time and having absolutely no understanding of it all. I mostly struggled with a deep and threatening disappointment in myself. Was I oversensitive? I was mad and confused for letting this affect me so much, but I felt stuck in a pool of sadness nonetheless.

I go to work in a haze every day now, like a zombie but with emotions. I am lifeless but burning inside. It's exhausting and I want it to stop. To switch it off. I want to not care.

I've decided it's time to see a proper psychologist. I found one in Hatfield. I have no idea what a psychologist is supposed to achieve, and how I'm supposed to know if this guy is good at his job or not, but he is close by and he is cheap. I feel better at the thought of feeling better. I hope the treatment works and that I will continue to feel good for a long time after.

## Age 25

I have asked Justin to marry me. We have been seeing each other on and off for a while. The last time we broke up, we stayed out of touch for six months and then I sent him a text to propose. He said yes.

We get along well. He is nineteen years older than me and that's mostly the reason why we kept breaking up. The age difference kind of freaked me out a bit. Now, I realise that this may be my only chance to fit in and feel safe. I think I can be happy. It will probably make my parents proud too. A win-win situation.

## Age 26

Yesterday I spoke to Justin at what used to be *our* house. He threw his ring at me. He is nauseous with shock that I want a divorce. He asked me to collect my stuff tomorrow while he is at work. I get it. I asked him to keep the ring, but he doesn't want it, so I took it with me. I don't know what I am supposed to do with it.

Almost a month at Crescent Clinic, which is basically a loony bin, gave me a lot of time to think. I landed up there while Justin was on one of his work trips. My sister had found me passed out on the floor of our lounge with an overdose of depression. The world was dead to me. She put me to bed and sat next to me, and when I woke up I confessed that I needed help.

I spent the first three days at the clinic hiding in bed. I hate groups, I am afraid of people, and talking to strangers makes me panic even though I disguise it well. But I had no resources left to disguise *anything*, so I slept.

On the third day, the managing therapist dragged me out of bed because I had to see my psychiatrist and psychologist once a day and I had already missed three days. I was also forced to do group sessions.

The therapy helped and the psychiatrist told me I was bipolar, which was why none of the antidepressants had ever worked. You can't treat bipolar with that kind of medication, he said. I needed a mood stabiliser, so he gave me about three different ones, as well as antianxiety meds and sleeping pills.

I feel like I have cataracts in my eyes because they are constantly glazed over from the drugs. But at least I don't feel anything else.

The day I was released, Justin fetched me and dropped me at my parents'. He had to do something after, he said. I had not seen him in the longest time. I felt a bit abandoned when he just left me like that. I was deeply saddened by it. I kept thinking about my conversations during therapy and how I had discovered that getting a divorce was the right thing to do because there was nothing worse than feeling displaced *and* imprisoned. But how could I get divorced and risk disappointing my family – especially my dad – again? I was still thinking about all that when my dad found me in my old bedroom that same day, trying to distract myself with a book. 'Dawjees don't carry baggage,' he said to me. And that was all the permission I needed to ask for a divorce.

## Age 27

I have come to Stellenbosch University to study my honours in journalism. I have always wanted to be a writer, and I feel like I should get some distance from this life, from Pretoria, the city that feels like it broke me, and go do that.

My acceptance letter came through at a time when there was once again a lot of tension in the house. After the divorce I moved back home, but I have been living on my own for too long and I forgot what these miserable moments were like.

After working at the school for five years, I cashed out my retirement annuity. It was a good amount. Enough for a few months' rent at a garden cottage, fees for the year, textbooks and a minimal living subsidy.

By the time I left, my relationship with my dad was on the mend a bit and he came with us to the airport. I was emotional. I felt homeless and uprooted again. In that moment I found strength in thinking that maybe the only thing that would bring me closer to my father was being really far away.

I needed a new start. Just like I needed a new car. I wrote off the Citi Golf my dad bought me by trying to drive off a highway bridge because I was depressed and didn't want to live any more. My cashed-out RA was enough for a new ride too.

91

I flushed all my meds a while before that 'driving off a bridge' incident because I was tired of explaining myself to my family and being castigated about my mental health 'problems' and my unnecessary medication. I wanted to be strong without the chemicals. But … I am pretty sure I would have done the car thing anyway. I am hoping Stellenbosch will breathe life back into me.

## Age 29

My relationship with my dad has improved tenfold, but now I am moving back to Gauteng. I can't believe I am moving back to Gauteng. At least it's Joburg and not Pretoria. Pretoria is a curse to me.

When I graduated at Stellenbosch I won a writing competition with the *YOU* magazine family. That included *DRUM* and *Huisgenoot*. The prize was R50 000 and a job at their Cape Town office for a year. I was happy in the Western Cape and desperate to stay, so the job opportunity at the magazine was a saving grace. I didn't have any money left. Being a student eats through a retirement fund pretty quickly.

Three other students 'won' with me. That wasn't supposed to be the case, but they did. They got jobs as well. I got the money, which paid my rent for the next year, but I also received more racism at that place than I could stomach. No racism is worth R50 000.

That's why I am leaving for my dream job as social media editor at the *Mail & Guardian*.

## Age 30

I have taken time off work. My boss has been wonderful and supportive. My world is washed in black and white. I cannot see in colour and I lie in a ball on the couch, unable to control my crying. My sister allows me to chain-smoke, feeds me tea and makes sure that I eat at least a bowl of soup every now and then.

## Age 31

I am seeing someone and it is terrifying. I am so confused in this relationship. She is white and I am always tussling with myself about my place in the relationship. There isn't a day that goes by that does not make me feel like I am being used as a political badge of honour. This could happen, right?

This person is on a black-consciousness journey even though she is white, and I don't think I am cut out to be her educator. It is difficult and it gets more difficult every day because I constantly have to operate within the boundaries of her fragility.

Am I a trophy of her progressiveness? Am I a really bad person for not wanting to be her political crutch in this phase of her life before she finds her 'woke' feet?

Sometimes I think maybe she does not like me at all. Only the experience of me. Virtue signalling.

Is this the price all people of colour must pay in interracial relationships?

## Age 32

Thank god I am back in Cape Town. Nothing cleanses me more than this city. My new medication is helping as well. After four years of not treating my illness, I finally went to a really great doctor at the Donald Gordon clinic in Joburg. I also found an awesome therapist. Both of them met me at another deeply suicidal time in my life.

A couple of days after returning from a holiday, the partner who seemed to be having an identity crisis broke up with me. At the same time, I was heading down depression lane. I had been on that road for a long time already, and I wondered how much longer I would remain there because of the break-up.

Nothing is scarier than standing on a balcony and feeling the most pathetic you have ever felt because you cannot find the courage to throw yourself off it.

I got so desperate that night on the balcony that I even called the suicide hotline thinking, on some messed-up level, that talking to them would help convince me to just end it all. It didn't. It had the opposite effect. And god bless the woman who answered the phone at the call centre that night.

I didn't jump, but I started cutting. Deeply. I had never done this to myself before. The cuts were so bad at one stage that I probably needed a stitch or two, but I never saw a doctor about it. I was too embarrassed. The wounds festered a bit. I wrapped my arms in long sleeves for a very long time to hide the weakness that left scars on my deltoids.

I spent my days feeling like I wanted to jump out of my skin. Like I was an alien in a strange universe who no one understood. I felt like I personally didn't understand anything or anyone either. I felt like I had no roots, and no place in this world. I wasn't of it and I wasn't for it.

That's what drove me to my new psychiatrist and therapist.

My doctor told me I am most certainly not bipolar. I am a depressive who suffers from a lack of emotional resilience. He explained new studies in neuroscience – brain pathways, that sort of thing. He gave me a mood stabiliser, an antidepressant and a 'for emergencies only' anxiety pill. The medication is really working. He also introduced me to mindfulness. I like it. It helps me check out of a situation whenever I need to. It's not something that would ever have appealed to me before, but now I find myself practising it all the time.

I am about to start my new job in Cape Town as a programme manager for impactAFRICA, a grant fund for data journalism.

## Age 32

I met Rebecca Davis three weeks ago. I have never felt this way before. This feeling is so new. A whole lot of new. And so lovely. We've only known each other for twenty-one days, but we really want to get married and spend forever together. The wedding is in December.

My parents are coming. They have accepted our union and given us their blessing. This makes me so happy. My dad is even giving a speech. That makes me even happier.

## Age 33

Rebecca is on the couch. I am on the bed. My meds are in my belly. Charlie, our cat, is running laps between us. And when the depression comes again, and it will, at least I will feel I have roots and I can plant my feet firmly on the ground. I am home. *We* are home.

# Why I'm down with
## *Downton Abbey*

I am afraid of white people. It doesn't matter what class they are, it doesn't matter what job they do, it doesn't matter if I am paying to stay at a hotel in Europe and they are cleaning the floor in the foyer to lay a shiny path before me, I still recoil in fear at their very presence. And so I take pleasure in watching *Downton Abbey*. Fearlessly.

When *Downton Abbey* premiered, the website *Gawker* released a list of reasons why the show is so good.

Reasons like this:

- *It's highbrow.* It deals with issues like the women's movement in the twentieth century, and the sinking of the *Titanic*.
- *It's lowbrow.* It has all the right ingredients for a Bollywood soapie but with better-timed close-ups. It has secrets, gossip, rumours, affairs, engagements, disengagements, etc.
- *It has good heroes and better villains.* (I won't get into this. The *Gawker* explanation was a bit of a stretch.)
- *It has insults.* Now this I can fully agree with. The scriptwriting is exquisitely decorated with some of the best slights and slurs I have ever come across. They mostly fall from the mouth of the countess, played by Maggie Smith.

The *Gawker* piece must have been written by a white person, given that the list failed to include the obvious: *Downton Abbey* completely lacks diversity. It forgot to mention that it portrays white privilege in all its morning glory. It's a show that asks the viewer to get lost in the luxury of a white twentieth-century England and forget that, during the same time, black people, Asian people, all kinds of people who weren't white, were busy being displaced – or worse.

I have a lot of friends who refuse to watch it for these very reasons. It is a white show for white people.

Months after the *Gawker* article was posted, the critical analyses started pitching up on Google searches. The representation question was raised and answered. The show's producers argued that the depiction of a more diverse society would be historically incorrect. And you know what, I agree. There is nothing worse to me than having a token black person – in any situation. And you just know that that's how they're going to 'diversify'. Instead of fighting stereotypes, they end up perpetuating them. The token black person is always the assistant or the singer or the athlete or the adopted sibling from an underprivileged background. In fact, they eventually introduced a black singer in season four, but we'll chat about that another day.

In the case of another hit show I adore – *Friends* – the eventual emergence of the show's black character comes in the form of Charlie, a professor of palaeontology who dates Ross. Charlie is the whitest black woman I have ever seen. And no, it's not because she is an academic or educated or a professional or any of those things. She is whiter than Rachel because there is nothing culturally black about her. This, to me, is the worst kind of inclusion. And these things happen because the people who are striving for diverse casts so that they can garner diverse audiences are white.

Good on the producers of *Downton*, I say. There would be nothing worse than pretending like the folks at the abbey were left-wing revolutionaries who welcomed one and all into their shire of equality – if not economically then at least racially. Good on the producers for not making it so. Tokenism is more offensive than exclusion.

*Downton Abbey* is a show I love to watch, and here's why:

- I love the golden retriever whose yellow coat is as manicured as the lawns. He is cute, shame.
- I love Maggie Smith's dowager countess. She is a legend and one day entire books will be written about her wisecracks.
- I love the milky-white minions who scurry about and make tea and bake bread and polish shoes and saddle horses.

In conclusion, I love watching *Downton Abbey* because it is a series about white aristocrats with their white slaves and it makes for pretty cathartic viewing. Plain and simple.

But, despite all my *Schadenfreude*-fuelled feistiness when I have the protection of a screen, put me in front of a white person in real life and I cower. This isn't just my own insecurity, I've learnt. It's an actual pathology.

Monnica Williams, a psychologist, professor and former director of the University of Louisville's Center for Mental Health Disparities, conducted a study on race-based trauma. It's a field begging for more exploration, but research is short on academic papers purely because it needs to be conducted by people of colour in order to have true meaning and effect, and there is still a lack of opportunity for this demographic in academic circles. Williams found that race-based trauma is

a natural byproduct of the types of experiences that minorities have to deal with on a regular basis. I would argue that it is pathological, which means it is a disorder that we can assess and treat. To me, that means these are symptoms that are a diagnosable disorder that require a clinical intervention.

We fail to recognise these symptoms as part of a disorder because the post-traumatic stress of racism and the effects of what I call 'white-perfection propaganda' are so intrinsic. It has become so normalised and natural in the cellular memory of people of colour. We often don't see it as a problem at all. We just accept the world we live in.

Being a person of colour scares me. I make myself small. I move through the world making exhaustive efforts to be invisible. In the face of white strangers, I lower my gaze. I speak when I am spoken to. I make cowardly eye contact only to greet politely, smile, nod and show respect. I do this with more effort than necessary and then lower my gaze again. This anxiety is my status quo and the status quo for many people of colour. Please can we just take a second to realise how fucked up that is? Really. How fucked up is it that this politeness is not the offspring of pure courtesy — as it should be — but rather the spawn of fear. Fear of degradation, criticism and conflict. If we aren't polite, we cannot prove our humanity. We are undeserving of being treated with dignity and respect in the face of adversity unless we bow our heads and kneel.

How fucked up is it that history taught us to despise ourselves? That from the moment we open our eyes, we see a white world. A world in which we have no real place. A world where we are displaced because the media and actual events have drilled into us that we have no real power. We have been punctured by this idea that we are undeserving. We are even undeserving of the privilege of protection from the police. This may seem like an American problem, but it isn't.

The police have never bullied me and I live in an environment where their forces are black and I should feel some kind of kinship with them, yet I still fear them. When covering the State of the Nation Address in 2017, things turned sour. Stampedes, angry crowds and trigger-happy police officers were rife. The enforcers were happy to launch smoke bombs. The air was filled with chasing and cries and banging and bright sparks of fire. Rebecca and I ran too. And after detaching ourselves from a wall while covering each other's eyes because we thought the smoke might be teargas, my (white) partner sought a sense of safety by standing with the riot police.

At the sight of this, I went into fight-or-flight mode. Her decision was threatening to me. My evolutionary response was to grab her and run away from them. As journalists, we often find ourselves in situations that call for barbed-wire barricades and armed police patrols. She often tells me about her sense of comfort and safety at their presence. I always disagree and voice my fear.

In his 1962 essay 'Letter from a Region in My Mind', writer and social critic James Baldwin wrote: 'White people hold the power, which means that they are superior to blacks (intrinsically, that is: God decreed it so), and the world has innumerable ways of making this difference known and felt and feared.' No truer words have been spoken or written.

I don't encounter the same fear when in the company of black people, South American people, Asians, Arabs, etc. When travelling to their countries, there is a degree of affinity and sincere respect, which is unspoken but understood regardless of class or education. This was not my experience in Germany, for instance, where the reality of an age-old lesson hit me in the face. White people are considered better at everything just because they are white, and so the world teaches us to worship them. A hard thing to admit. But the seed of this sermon has been planted in all of us.

When a white person marries a person of colour, they are looked down upon. It is assumed that they settled for less. When a person of colour has a white partner, however, even their own people revere them. 'They married up' is a popular slogan.

A lack of historical racial education abandons us to sickening insecurity. The 'woke' renaissance eradicates or tries to escape the reality of this inferiority complex. It is weak to talk about this inheritance now. And even though I have started paying attention to this, and I'm constantly aware of it anxiously flowing through my veins as I move through the world, I still subconsciously accept what the world has taught me even though I do not believe it: whites are exemplary. This ideology still dictates my behaviour in many ways. But when I am home, watching *Downton Abbey*, I have free reign over my reaction. I can put my true beliefs into action. Instead of bowing, kneeling and begging, I can safely stand, point, laugh and even judge if I want to. And seeing white underlings scamper about sets my subconscious free. Watching *Downton Abbey* is a form of free therapy. Cowardly. But free.

Trendy hashtags of empowerment like #SelfLove and #Black-GirlMagic make us feel momentarily stronger, but in reality they have become one of the many offerings to calm the waters of our minds. They are a mechanism to arm our psychologies so we can fear less physically.

And then, of course, there are 'woke' white people who seek to convince us that we have less to fear from them. They do us favours, but then have the audacity to preach about equality and rainbow-nationness. Their freedoms and entitlement are so vast that they share with pride their fragility and struggles of being white.

Someone I once thought of as a friend had the cheek to shed white tears in the presence of myself and another friend of colour because she felt discriminated against on account of her race. Her inability to recognise that even *that* performance came with a healthy degree of privilege and power enraged me so much that I went home and cried for hours. It was insensitive and hateful. It sickened me, and I sickened myself some more, because in the face of all that whiteness I was still afraid. I was aware of her fragility and did not want to hurt her feelings. This is insane. It is insane that I carry the truth in the back of my throat and lug it home to be expressed in isolation. It infuriates me. She infuriated me. And even though I have become better at telling people like that that they are ridiculous, I have not mastered the courage or the language.

Pseudo-Bikos, I see you. I see you with your militancy. I see you ready yourselves. You've removed your rings and placed your berets of millennial wokeness neatly on the hat stand. Beat me with your words of righteousness if you must. Often I am in need of that fire. I wish constantly that only a part of me were like you, even though I do not believe in shouting at the world all the time. But I also no longer believe in suffering in silence to protect white emotions any more.

I will say one thing loud and proud when it comes to *Downton Abbey*: wokeness schmokeness and diversity schmiversity. You won't watch a show without any black people in it? It's for white people? I get it. But *Downton Abbey* doesn't need racial representation in order for me to like it. Instead of boycotting a show without black people in it, I choose to watch a show where, for a change, the people doing the menial work aren't black and I can be filled with glee and giggles as the whites do blue-collar work. I can openly and with confidence feel superior for a change. I do not have to wade through centuries of embedded racial insecurity that began long before my 'transformed' world and exists within me still.

# My Islamic state of mind

The University of Pretoria is a segregated black hole waiting to swallow lost souls and outcasts. And I don't just mean in the obvious black-and-white racial sense. I mean when it comes to intra-racial and intra-cultural discrimination. It is the actual worst. The only thing I give it credit for? It's where I met my best friend.

If I hated school – and I did – I hated varsity even more. I did not enjoy the masses of people walking from point A to point B to settle in hall A or hall B where someone could talk at them instead of with them. I did not enjoy that it had structure but also no structure. I definitely did not enjoy being told what to learn, or what made some work good and some work bad and why the hell other people got to decide that. I was also academically paralysed by what I am convinced is ADHD and a life-threatening allergy to formal education. I made use of the library; abused it. I read all kinds of books on all kinds of things. I wrote all the exams because I had to, and when things required critical thinking, discussion or debate, I went to class. When I wasn't doing any of these things, I was pissing off the Muslim students' association by just being me, and smoking cheap dope. *Kassam*, hell hath no fury like a rich Indian Muslim from Laudium at the University of Pretoria.

The Indian Muslims at UP were all from Laudium, but we attended different schools and so we hadn't grown up together. You know? Not in the way that comes from living in a close-knit community. There were rich kids who lived on the avenues up on the hill. They were constantly surrounded by other students who were also Muslim and wealthy. They got what they wanted when they wanted it. The only thing we got in my family, whether we wanted it or not, was more education.

In my heavenly little portion of Laudium, I was surrounded by Hindu, Tamil, Christian and Muslim kids of a lower economic demographic. We played on the street and used all the neigh-bours' houses for hide-and-seek. A cooldrink was a weekend delicacy because our parents were strict, but those rich Indian Muslim students got Coke in their baby bottles. Lush. Everything in their lives was lush, except their minds. Like their view of the world, which included only cookie-cutter versions of themselves with the same beliefs and thoughts, their minds were small.

We didn't even grow up with the same religious teachings. Where they attended conventional madrassas, my siblings and I received most of our religious education at home. Every Sunday night, my dad read and explained the Quran to us verse by verse (in English), and we were made to engage in analytical discourse so as to understand the philosophical meaning of spirituality. We also explored interpretations of the text and studied it in a historical and factual manner.

Many madrassas only teach students how to recite the Quran in Arabic, without teaching them the language itself. So while these learners may know how to repeat an extract – or the entire scripture – from memory, they often don't know what they're saying. Pair this with a teacher who is probably brainwashing students into believing that Islam is monolithic, and what you've got is a cult. Or at least that's how I think of it. So by the time I got to university, that's exactly what I faced in the other Muslim students: a cult who believed their own distorted truths about Islam and kept to themselves. I possessed no key to this community.

Laudium was once a whites-only area known as Claudius, after Claudius Marais de Vries, a former mayor of Pretoria. In 1961, the apartheid government declared the small suburb an Indian township. It aimed to house people specific to this ethnic group so that they could be evacuated from Marabastad and central Pretoria and be segregated from other ethnic groups. At the same time, Marabastad and Central Pretoria were, of course, zoned as white areas following the implementation of the Group Areas act.

I don't know why Laudium is called Laudium or who named it that. What I do know is that it's derived from the Latin word *laus*, which means 'to praise'. Laudium (or laudanum) was also a drug in the Victorian era, popularly consumed by the working class. On the streets, it was known as 'blue troll ass dust' and 'evening delight'. Doctors prescribed it for anything from pain to tuberculosis, and Victorian nursemaids even used it to calm cranky infants (often leading to their untimely deaths).

Fun urban legend: my grandfather used to say that Laudium was called 'Ghost Town' because it was built on a massive gravesite. There is no research to support this, but it's a cool story and I spent a lot of my childhood digging for human remains.

Fun fact from Wikipedia: in 1981, Umkhonto we Sizwe launched a rocket attack on the Voortrekkerhoogte military base from Laudium, and the homes of local politicians in Laudium who supported apartheid were bombed.

Anyway, that's where our parents and our grandparents went, away from the city and into the township, along with their friends – Christian, Muslim, Hindu, all of them, as long as the government could classify them as 'Indian'. Then came us. And then, in about 1990, came the proposals to develop private schools. Hotshots in the Muslim community clubbed together to start a private Islamic school. (Well, that's how it started in my head. I don't know the economic details; I was six.) The school would incorporate all the strictest teachings of the Dïn (religion) into its syllabus. Obviously this included stuff like wearing hijab and having no co-ed classes, ever. It was a private school, so it was expensive. Forget that the Quran literally says that education is the right of all individuals and the moral duty of every capable individual. No, only economically capable individuals could go to this school. I did not attend.

It was only at Tuks that I encountered this bunch of bourgeois snobs who drove their daddies' BMWs, wore only Guess or Diesel, and walked the moral high ground just because they went to a private Muslim school. This basically meant that any young woman who was sort of semi-athletic, smoked, wore jeans and hoodies all the time, kept her hair relatively short and never bothered to straighten it, and dared to study music of all things, was basically the devil. If eyes could stone, I would have been under Table Mountain. It did not help my cause that I mostly hung out with male friends who were either black, white, coloured or Hindu; none of them Muslim. I was never going to date – or marry – a good Muslim boy. Not from this community, what with all our differences in beliefs and me being such a rebel.

Their exclusive, judgemental version of Islam and outlook on life also made me hate being Muslim. I never could understand why I needed to believe in a god who hated me. Who was just waiting to judge me. Who gave other people the right to think they were better than me and could judge me too? How did any of that make someone good? Wasn't the point of any religion to make you a respectful, humble human being with good morals and principles? To treat people fairly and equally? This was not the impression I got from the Cardbox Clan, as I called them, because they were soft, shifty and loved their mental boxes.

The Clan hung out on the corner of the piazza in front of the First National Bank ATM. The piazza housed the main cafeteria on campus, along with some eateries and, of course, the 'coffee shop'. This is where they held court. You needed ovaries of steel to walk in there and order a subpar caffeine drink. Every time I queued at that till to pay the lovely Portuguese lady, I felt the eyes on my back. Caesar had it easy.

One day I made my way up and a tall woman who always intrigued me stopped me before the ATM. She was part of the Cardbox Clan, but I always thought she stood out. She didn't seem to be made of cardboard, and she definitely did not seem like she fit into any of their preconceived boxes. Her name was Rasheda Titus. And I was 100 per cent right in all my assumptions about her. Rasheda is now my best friend and the oracle of my life.

Rasheda will deny this story, but it is absolutely true. She stopped me that day to hover over me (she is very tall) and ask me whether my eyes were my own. I do have a stunning pair of eyes, if I may say. A pool of chocolate, I tell you. Or the eyes of a swamp rat with brown cataracts. I said, 'Yes, they are real.' She was completely entranced and became my BFF. And that's that, only it isn't. We spent the rest of our tertiary education days together, socialising more and more. Hanging out. It wasn't long before the Cardbox Clan had had enough and decided Rasheda needed an intervention. In their eyes, she was naive and had no idea how evil I was. She needed to be warned of the terrible Muslim who was crap at convention.

Rasheda told me this, but only years later because that's the type of person she is. If she did not believe in something, there was no reason to speak it. I noticed that she hung out with the Cardbox Clan less, but I never enquired. Our friendship grew; no warning was needed. In spite of hanging out with people who I thought were indoctrinated and spent their days judging everything that wasn't like them, she stuck around and they accepted her. Rasheda is a tall, coloured woman with alopecia. She has a single mom who remarried, so she has five additional siblings. She checked none of the Clan's boxes. But her Islam is a religion of love, and her choice to love rather than judge made her accepting and easy to accept.

We've spent the last fifteen years challenging each other, learning, growing, cleaning up each other's mistakes and crying. Rasheda ended up marrying a guy I sort of dated when I was in tenth grade. I always joke that I love her so much that I had to make sure she was in good hands. She is. They have the most beautiful relationship and together we have the most beautiful extended family. I have seen her exit the orthodox, Islamic-school way of thinking and gravitate into Sufism. She has seen me become less and less of a practising Muslim, with all its rules and rigour, and watched me find peace.

I have never had a relationship more spiritual than this one, and if this is her Islamic state of mind, then it is mine too.

# My mother, the true radical

My mom is a tough woman. She's independent, she's feisty and she doesn't suffer fools. She can pack more into one day than I could accomplish in a week: run a household, manage my dad's office, throw in a yoga class and still have time to bake biscuits – if she feels like it.

Call her a feminist, though, and she might just have a heart attack. Yet to me, she embodies a type of feminism we don't hear much about. She's strong. She's creative. But she is also a product of patriarchy and prejudice. She has not been subjected to the physical abuse a lot of women suffer, but because of the place that society carved out for her, she chose, in many ways, to be timid while I was growing up. In order to survive, she maintained a degree of invisibility and a reluctance to challenge authority.

That's not considered politically progressive by our modern feminist standards.

In science, there's a particle called the free radical. These are atoms or groups of atoms that are highly chemically reactive, even towards each other – not unlike a particular type of militant feminist I've come across in my generation. Like those mercurial particles, these feminists are often reactive instead of introspective, whether the context is a university lecture, social media or a chat with friends.

I have seen these 'free radicals' criticise other women for not being feminist enough, not being powerful enough, not exerting their agency enough. The 'Why doesn't she just leave?' statement often uttered by the allegedly more enlightened and liberated woman in reference to the domestically abused one is a mild example. For some feminists, women should just do better.

There is a place for the spontaneous combustion of feminism's free radicals. They play an important regulatory role in many social circumstances. If all women turned the other cheek and condoned the notion that 'daddy beats me because he loves me', well, we might still be normalising things like physical abuse and rape.

Free radicals help all kinds of women rage against the thinking that we should sympathise with men as their power is challenged and try to understand their pain before we criticise them for abusing women. In many instances, they make space for the voices of the silent.

But, while their volatile nature is necessary, it lacks empathy and respect when it comes to *all* women. The feminists I'm talking about would probably look at a woman like my mother with pity. If they heard that she still lays out my father's clothes for him every morning, they'd get busy planning a hostage rescue. That's patronising bullshit.

As a Muslim woman of colour in South Africa, my mother has had to face a multitude of stratums and facets that define her as a woman in her society. As a result of this, she has had to find her own type of feminism. She has had to navigate the roles of women in terms of racism, tradition, religion, and cultural and societal norms. Women of colour are not just facing sexism; they're battling all these other things at the same time. Their activism requires them to jump many hurdles before even engaging with the feminism we know today. Their version of feminism may seem lost and unrecognisable to our politically advanced eye, but the role they play in the fight for feminism is real and requires acknowledgement, even if it may seem passive or silent.

I often think about these issues when I watch *The Color Purple* (1985), the film adaptation of Alice Walker's 1982 novel of the same name. *The Color Purple* is my go-to movie when I need catharsis. I own the DVD and pop it in often. In the most stressful moments of my life, when I feel burdened with the challenges of being a woman, I succumb to the comfort of watching it. I love to relive that story over and over again. It makes my problems as a woman seem small, and it gives me perspective on the forgotten burdens that other women still face.

My opinion of *The Color Purple* is unconventional. I don't think Alice Walker wrote the book for people like me to use as some sort of therapy, but the culmination of events in the life of the lead character is a significant and important message when it comes to women in the home. Women who have no time to think about the politics of feminism (the waves, the movement, the meaning). Feminism doesn't exist in theory in these women's lives. It lives in practice.

The main character is Celie, a young black woman whose life lacks the freedom of choice. We are witness to this from the beginning. She gives birth to two children because her father rapes her. She cannot choose whether to keep her kids or give them up for adoption – he decides for her and they are taken away. To her father, Celie is a burden. To rid himself of this burden he decides that she is to marry a widower and take care of his house and children. The widower is warned that Celie is 'spoiled'. She also does not check any of the standard boxes of beauty: she has 'bad' hair and very dark skin, for example. Constant societal castigation leaves her with only one option: shut up, never smile, do all of this to survive, practise strength by submitting to physical abuse.

In the first half of the movie, it becomes clear that women like Celie cannot simply abandon their situations in search of a better life. It's not easy to accept this. When I watched the film with Rebecca, who had never seen it before, she voiced her frustration with Celie: 'Why doesn't she just leave?' Rebecca is an outspoken feminist, and I understand this take on things. I was really young the first time I watched it, and as an angst-ridden teen whose upbringing made me aware of the power of women and what we should not put up with, I shared the same anger towards Celie.

Why did Celie choose to stay? Why did she actively subject herself to isolation and degradation? I admit, a big part of me ignorantly thought, *Well fine. If she won't do anything about it, she deserves it.* This belief lacks understanding and stems from the idea that women who will not do anything about their situations deserve what they get. This is an anti-feminist stance that many people believe to be feminist. It condones the abuse and disrespect of women who are not as fortunate as we are. Women who do not get to protest the abuse that befalls them because their path to liberation looks very different.

To be a feminist on the ground, to publicly voice dissent against norms, advocate for women's rights and fight for the equality of the sexes is unfortunately not an option for all women. One woman's practice of feminism is not necessarily another's. Without considering the important role of intersectionality, the feminist fight is driven by ignorance instead of support.

The first wave of feminism, which focused on the fight for suffrage, produced a homogeneous view of feminism and women's experiences. When this wave ended, the second wave of feminism took off in the early 1960s in the United States. Twenty years later, it started to gain traction in Europe and Asia. But it ignored the significant role of intersectionality, which remains an important social theory that acknowledges the fact that not all women or feminists are white, from the same economic or religious background or able-bodied, for example.

First- and second-wave feminism ignored the fact that, for people like Celie, the path to feminism and the experience of it were very different to a white woman's at the time. While Celie was a slave of patriarchy, the white woman had progressed. She had the right to drive, vote and have a say in the household, to an extent. Over and above the fact that white women in the film did not have to pander to the expectations of patriarchy in the home by doing the cooking and cleaning (because people of colour did it for them), they absolutely did not have to pander to the needs of other races. We see this in the mayor's wife, whose disposition is starkly different to Celie's. She's relatively more independent, she's verbose and bossy, and she is not threatened by a predominantly male society. In the middle of town she demands that Sophia (a woman of colour) come and work for her. She does not consider Sophia's own strength and independence when she refuses. It is not allowed. Sophia is out of line. Her attitude is out of line.

Today, we still ignore intersectionality and the layered, dynamic struggle of some women compared to others.

*The Color Purple* asks us to consider the actions of women who are more vulnerable than others. It argues that the choice of directing their own lives is not the same as for someone who falls in a less vulnerable category. Who maybe comes from a place

where culture, tradition, religion and race are not prominent iden-
tifiers when it comes to their roles. For less privileged women,
the rights of sexuality, family, work, how they should be treated
in the workplace, reproductive choice and the option of joining
the military, to name a few, do not belong to them. Not yet. The
film's emphasis is on the fight for a woman's choice, and how that
might look different from our own.

In simple terms, there is no singular, cookie-cutter feminism.

We did not suddenly emerge as 'woke' feminists. We are the
products of previous generations' prolonged and fragmented conversations. We are the stuff of painful challenges that live silently
in the minds of these struggling women. We have been harvested
from their internal rage. We have witnessed them try to break free
of insufferable prisons defined by chores – the ironing of the
clothes, the washing of the dishes, the being at the beck and
call of their husbands. These are not superfluous conflicts. These
are not shallow stereotypes to overcome even though it's easy to
categorise them as such today.

These women are our mothers, our aunts, our grandmothers.
They are even our sisters, existing in our same generation.

They live out their lives in stillness, while we 'progressive'
women flick our middle fingers at their confines. Their sound-
less struggle has become our noisy protest. They darn the socks
and raise the kids. They cook, clean, play the disciplinarian. Their
fight is for the peace to get by. We spew poison at their expense
because we think we are so different, so much... better. And
while we *have* progressed, I have to ask: is it feminist to disregard
and degrade the experiences of one generation of women over
another's? Or have we become the female versions of our patriarchal counterparts? Unable to empathise and quick to judge?

It seems to me that we regard theirs as a cumbersome life

too uncool for us to acknowledge. We forget that women like this still exist. They keep things peaceful so that the patriarchy remains comfortable and calm, maybe because they fear it, but also to make things easier on themselves. For these women, staying safe within the status quo is winning the fight.

My upbringing was comparatively feminist. My grandfather and father raised me, my sister and brother with a strong sense of admiration for womanhood and the important role women play in society. My mother had no such luck. And even though the current fight for feminism is as important as ever, to me it still seems so small when I compare it, generationally, to the fight of those before, who still suffer the consequences now.

Despite Beyonce's 2014 announcement that girls 'Run the World', girls and women don't. Pop-culture references to women's social roles may influence a select few, but broader patterns of power remain unchanged. Girls *can* run the world, but we don't. Glib proclamations of female power should be challenged, yet because they fit a certain trendy model of what 'women slaying' looks like, they are celebrated.

In contrast to the worship that accompanied Beyonce's 'Run the World', compare the feminist reaction to J.Lo's chart-topping hit 'Ain't Your Mama'. The song is about how women are more than housekeepers and mothers. They are not defined solely by their children, their husbands and their chores.

It was criticised for trying to be a feminist manifesto because the video portrays female stereotypes, even though it proceeds to bash them. 'Weak', it was called. 'Regressive', even. This despite the fact that the whole video is basically a big fuck you to patriarchy and being barefoot-in-the-kitchen, and plays out scenes of rebellion – a woman dropping a home-cooked dinner on her husband's head, for example. This kind of mutiny was criticised for being irrelevant in the current discourse. It was not political enough. Not contemporary enough. It lacked 'substance', wrote Christina Cauterucci, a staff writer for *Slate*.

Cauterucci went on to write that the portrayal of feminism in the lyrics and video sticks to

> a conservative idea of gender equality that rests on petty comebacks against lazy husbands, leering bosses, and inattentive boyfriends. It's a cute shtick when it roots itself in the mid-century fight against the image of a domestic, subservient maid-as-wife. But the song's premise – a woman refusing to cook and launder for her husband, because she 'ain't [his] mama' – continues into modern urban life. Set against that backdrop, the idea of a woman proudly demanding that her husband wash his own underwear, as if it's some kind of revolutionary feminist act, grates the senses.

Grates the senses? A mid-century fight? These kinds of narrow views suggest that the writer and other critics forget that the nucleus of patriarchy is in the home, and it is in 'stereotypes' like the above that feminism comes alive and is most necessary. While many of us are 'waking up like this' in this day and age and having academic conversations, this kind of discourse is not accessible because, to these 'stereotypical' women, the 'new-age' arguments rest on what for them are armchair experiences. J.Lo's song may not represent the on-fleek feminism we get around every corner today – but it *is* real. I know this fight against archaic norms and gender roles. I've seen it, I have grown up with and around it. It has angered me. And it has enlightened me. There are, of course, problems with perpetuating these roles, but, as stated, feminism is not a one-size-fits-all thing. It's not a pair of those elasticated drawstring linen pants you can buy at Greenmarket Square.

*The Color Purple* portrays feminine stereotypes, male domination, the passive nature these women are forced to adopt and how these can be taken advantage of. But Alice Walker also gives us glimpses into the lives of more empowered, independent women than Celie, who challenge the patriarchy and gendered social norms around them. These women demand as much respect as they can within the constraints of the period. Very often, they get it. It's only because of the bond that Celie forms with these women, so different from her, that she is able to come into her own.

It's because of the quiet support from others that Celie gets angry, asserts herself and finally finds her voice in one of the most epic feminist scenes I have ever seen. 'You a low-down dirty dog, that's what's wrong,' she tells her husband, Albert. 'Time for me to get away from you, and enter into Creation. And your dead body'd be just the welcome mat I need.'

When Celie finds her voice, she starts to 'wear the pants', for lack of a better phrase. In fact, she ends up with her own store, Miss Celie's Folks Pants – where she literally makes pants for other women to wear too. It's a metaphor rooted, once again, in patriarchy, but still a significant victory in its context.

Celie eventually finding her voice is not an uncommon conclusion. My mom got mad too. She fought. She didn't shout. She struggled in silence for a long time, but ultimately she won. She stopped conforming to beauty norms, like dying her hair. Grey is taboo for Indian women. She took her life into her own hands. Now, if she wants to go to yoga in the middle of the day, she does. She does not allow herself to be bogged down by the idea that she has to be home to serve lunch. In her own way, she asserts her power and she is fearless. Maybe 'feminism' as we know it is the last thing on her mind, but it's feminism nonetheless.

Maybe we're not willing to accept Celie's or my mom's kind of feminism. Maybe they're not trendy. But my mother and other women like her are the molecules working at the root of patriarchal control day by day. They may not be 'free radicals', but they are true radicals.

# Tinder is a pocket full of rejection, in two parts

## PART 1

In Standard 4, when we still called them standards instead of grades and worked through an actual syllabus with real subjects that weren't all followed by the word 'literacy', I developed a friendship with a boy. A white boy. Let's call him Michael.

Michael was really good looking. And not in a weird 'OMG he is so cute' kind of way, but like properly cute. *Handsome.* It was the kind of beauty that wouldn't be going anywhere. It would not wobble with puberty or decline with age. There was no direction in which his features could one day fall that would render him stale bread. He was going to be forever young and gorgeous. I knew it then, and I know it now. I haven't seen him in decades, but I would bet my left nipple that he is still fine as hell.

Michael made braces look so good that you wanted braces too. And despite being a metal-mouth, he had the widest smile. His dimples were like warm hellos and his green eyes were like tiny, shiny Hartbeespoort dams. He had olive skin and chocolate-brown hair, but he was white. Definitely white.

On account of my own skin colour and the fact that I was a very intimidated minority, being friends with Michael was something I never even considered. It didn't bug me, and I never wished for it. It's just the way life is, I told myself. And I was okay with that. Although depressing, being at peace with a conclusion like that makes life in an all-white school easy. The days roll over and you roll with them, invisible.

All the gangs were friends with Michael. The sports gang. The super-clever gang. The talented drama crowd. And the most intimidating of all gangs: the blonde, Cobain-T-shirt-wearing gang. They stomped around in Doc Martens. They brought their Walkmans to sports days and blasted Green Day and Oasis and, obviously, Nirvana. They were always dressed in dark colours. They weren't goth. Just rebellious and cool. If Michael was untouchable, this crowd was omnipotent.

They swore all the time and stamped the Stüssy logo all over the school walls just because they could. They also knew what Stüssy was (it's a skateboard lifestyle brand). As someone who came from a very small, secluded community, I knew nothing about white things like this.

The girls were into modelling and lollipop eating. The guys were into throwing house parties and sneaking into their parents' liquor cabinets (I'm sure now that these stories were lies told to impress). And everyone was into everyone.

They were also bullies. And they bullied me often. They called me 'curry-muncher' and 'coolie'. Before meeting these kids, I had no idea what a curry-muncher was. At first I thought it might be some sort of endearing pet name. I went home one day and asked my grandfather. He explained its racist roots and I left it at that. I did not want to tell him I was being called that. It was too embarrassing.

They also practised less obvious methods of intimidation. They whispered and laughed at me in corridors in a way that makes you question whether it's really happening or if you're just going mad – until you see their side-eyes. The 'acting busy' and turning away from me when it came to selecting science-garden duty teams. And when the teacher assigned me to a group herself, it was always such a strain for them to have me around. No effort was made to hide the burden of my existence among the birds and the frogs.

I should also clarify: the majority of name-calling and bullying happened at the hands of the girls.

But then Spring Day came around and my luck changed. I was part of the team on science-garden duty that day. During class we got to feed the fish and the birds, and look at the lilies, I guess. It was boring. As a brown person I had no desire to put my hand in a pond thick with algae and catch tadpoles. But I had to pretend this thrilled me, so as to at least try to fit in a bit. The team I was on that week included some of the Cobain crew. The blondes and bullies. And Michael.

After some pottering about, the girls dared me to kiss Michael. He walked up to me as if on cue. Blushing and smiling, he kind of gave me the impression he wasn't going to be mean about it. And I really wanted to fit in. I wanted to be cool. Actually, I didn't really care about being cool. I just wanted to feel safe. I thought that by doing this, I would be left alone. So I said yes, fine. I acted all chill about it.

We stood next to the pond with, like, a metre between us and quickly pecked each other on the lips. We weren't quick enough, though. Our lips barely touched, but as soon as they parted the pointing and laughter began. Turns out, the time it takes to steal a kiss is more than enough time to snap a pic with a disposable camera. I was humiliated. Michael laughed along. I didn't know if he simply found it funny or if he was in on the deal to begin with. I didn't care. I only cared about the damn picture and where the hell it would end up. To be more specific, I worried about whether my parents would get hold of it through the malice of these demons. I worried about whether they would pull their whore child out of school and send me to an eternal detention of madrassa where my hair would never see the light of day. My little-girl balls started to sweat.

I lived in panic for the next few weeks. The picture was developed and made the rounds in class during that time. There was no way I could get my hands on it without making myself look like a bigger loser than I already was. I tried to act indifferent. It had not reached my parents yet. Maybe it would tear before it ever did, I thought.

Then it was sports day, and there was a 'fun walk' happening round one of the smaller fields. I was making my way there when Michael came up to me and asked if I would like to walk with him. I said yes. We walked a lap or two before he said he wanted to show me something. And just like that, he pulled the picture out of his pocket. He told me he had wanted it because he liked it and the other kids would stop passing it around now. I felt safe. Michael and I held hands and walked like that for the next few laps. I saw the Cobainers, the Stüssy stampers, the bullies. I saw them all, and for once I was the one with the side-eye.

But then a teacher on the sidelines called me from across the field. When I ran over, she shouted at me for holding Michael's hand. She told me I was brown and he was white and it wasn't okay. I was sinning. We could never mix. I was made to sit in class with her for the rest of the day. The field was right beside the window. Michael's life went on outside. And that's how long our friendship lasted. A few short laps. I went home with my secret and pretended to have an ordinary weekend. It could have been a lot worse, I guess.

On Monday, it was. I entered the school gate and found Michael standing there. I took it as a sign that Friday's debacle was over and it didn't mean anything. He didn't care about any of it and we would still be friends. I skipped (not really, but in my head I felt like I was skipping) towards him and smiled. But as I got closer I noticed he wasn't smiling back. He was laughing at me. He was laughing at me with the rest of them. And by *them* you know whom I mean. There was, however, one addition. Michael's mother. She had the picture and she asked me to please leave her son alone. She addressed me like I was dirty. Like I was the plague.

It later dawned on me that before she addressed me at the school gate, she had addressed the principal in his office. The message made the rounds faster than that damn photo. All the teachers watched me like a hawk. A restraining order of watchful eyes monitored my every move. I never so much as looked at Michael again.

It was a life lesson. I never dared show interest in or look at a white boy ever again. Not for the rest of primary school. Not in high school and certainly not at varsity. To them, I was still the plague. I was still dirty. They were better and I was not allowed to offend them with my interest. They would never be attracted to me, ever. Because of one plain fact: I was not white.

# PART 2

A few years ago, I found myself on a park bench in Perugia, Italy during the International Journalism Festival. A student came and sat next to me. She seemed older than an undergrad and wealthier as well. I made this deduction from her clothing: a stylish coat and a pair of brown leather Oxfords. To be fair, though, everyone in Italy is such a trendy dresser, it's hard to categorise their threads by class. I myself am a middle-class South African who often looks hobo-chic, in my opinion, without trying. No one in Italy looks hobo-chic. Not even in the Umbrian countryside where clothing stores are limited.

When I travel, one of my favourite things to do is find a public space and watch people while listening to music. Wearing a pair of cans on my ears makes my experience more relaxing. I can engage with the locals without actually having to engage. The earphones are a wonderful and subtle 'please don't talk to me' sign. It's a great way to make up tales about passers-by without ever having to listen to any of their talking. It's cheating, really.

The student took a minute to absorb the view of the valley below us before carefully setting up her water bottle in a reachable position. She pulled a Kindle from her bag and proceeded to read. My peripheral vision wandered instinctively towards the electronic page. The layout of the book seemed academic, but not too clinical. It was neat and minimalist. Not too text-heavy, but definitely non-fiction in its aesthetic.

The font was tiny and because books on Kindle open on the page you last read, I was unable to catch the title. Since human peripheral vision is blurry, I didn't try too hard to read any of it from my subtle side-eye glance. But when she swiped to the next page, my eyes caught the name of the new chapter: 'Relationships'. A pull quote just below screamed 'We need to stop letting information scare us'.

I smiled to myself. Whoever wrote this book had never met me. I was post-information-fear. I was out there, absorbing all the things about all the people. Sticks and stones could break my bones, but words definitely could not hurt me. Not like they did in a damn science garden years ago. I was invincible. I ... *I was on Tinder.*

I penned a mental ode to the wretched school kids: keep your tadpoles and your Cobain tees to yourselves; I have in my hands the power of the swipe. Oh, how times have changed. The world works in my favour now, I thought.

Tinder opens you up to a world of dating possibilities outside of what you would usually encounter. It is especially convenient for someone who doesn't like to go out to the clurrrrbs, and so is less likely to meet new people.

This is how Tinder works: you download the app and sign up. You upload up to six photos and a 500-word-max personal description. Descriptions can say anything from 'I love my car' to 'My wife is out with the baby, wanna hit it?' to the much more rare 'I am lovely, charming, employed, respectful and I am looking for my soul-mate because I just want someone to love'. When you're done with all of the above, you have a profile, which is visible to all other Tinder users in the vicinity.

This trip to Italy was the first time since a break-up that I was tempted to use the app. After careful consideration prior to departure, I figured Italy was a good place to start. I liked the idea of using Tinder as a novelty in a foreign country, and I could take it from there.

This gamified version of dating appealed to me for two reasons:
1. I had full control over the situation. I did not have to bat off annoying little flirt creatures that creepily lean in in real life. My phone. My pocket. My power.
2. I could expand my horizons. With the protection of the screen, I could test the white waters without any fear of drowning in the depths of race-based rejection.

The festival brought hundreds of people to Perugia. Statistically, my chances of matching with people were high. I could match up with either the locals or a variety of international media professionals from all over the world who were going to be in the town for as long as I was – about a week. I didn't want a long-term relationship. I wanted a social study in a technocratic age.

Tinder works hand in hand with Facebook. You can't sign up unless you have a Facebook profile. And by connecting with Facebook, the back-end of Tinder can do things like throw out possible matches for you based on your shared interests on Facebook. If both of you like *Pulp Fiction*, for example, and it is listed on your Facebook profile, that person will show up on Tinder as a possible match and you have the option to either swipe right (yes I like you) or left (no thanks, I am not here for this).

The focus question for my study, therefore, was: could Tinder decrease the likelihood of race-based rejection because the algorithm is set up to offer potential matches based on interests instead of racial preference? I was pretty positive I would find human beings evolved past the science-garden phase – even very shallowly. You didn't have to marry your match, but you could at least see beyond race and focus on your mutual interests.

I will add that my self-esteem when it came to white men had increased ten-fold since marrying a white man, although we divorced after six months because of our age difference. He was forty-one, I was twenty-six and he was the first white boyfriend I ever had. His interest in me occurred independent of any effort on my part. I did not have to convince him to like me in any way. I did not have to pretend I was anything I was not. I did not have to compromise the colour of my skin to feel accepted or more attractive to him. And just to be clear, I did not marry him *because* he was white. I married him because a lot of our interests matched. It was 2009. There was no Tinder. We had to figure the match thing out through actual face-to-face conversations.

Anyway, back to the experiment: all variables in the situation were perfect. Everything was set up for minimal emotional invest-ment. Not receiving a match is a lot less hurtful than someone telling you you're *kak* ugly because you're brown, for example. If I didn't get any matches, I could just continue swiping. On average, users spend about ninety minutes a day on Tinder, and log on around eleven times per day.

I cleaned up in Italy. As a woman of colour, I was impressed with the appearance politics of Italian men. I felt confident that my race was never taken into consideration when I received matches. Also, all my matches were heaps attractive. These were not desperate white losers who had to 'lower their standards to people of colour'. The world has convinced both us and them that this is a real thing.

My track record did not last long. A month later in Cape Town, the clean sweep turned into a shitstorm. In South Africa, I got no white matches. Appearance-based biases ruled all. We may have shared an interest in *Pulp Fiction*, but the superficial mattered more. Tinder in South Africa is nothing but fertile ground for race-based rejection. And this subliminal rejection hurts. In fact, it hurts more than rejection in person. It hurts more because it so strongly reaffirms the powers of exclusionary politics.

Tinder is, at its heart, a test of implicit bias. It sorely confirms the fact that subconscious prejudices are so deeply embedded in our cellular memory, so concretely moulded by society that there is no way for users to divorce themselves from what they've been told is attractive and what isn't. And beauty is white.

So pervasive is this belief in South Africa that, instead of subtly exercising their agency through a swipe, many people will state their racial preferences in their descriptions. I don't have to tell you, a lot of them look like this: 'No Asians. I'm not racist but whites only please.' Or: 'I have a lot of black friends, but I am only looking for white dates.'

Then, of course, we need to consider that the app is location-based. Areas like Cape Town are characterised by a whiter demographic, so the success rates for interracial matches decrease significantly because exclusionary politics increase so much. What does a brown girl have to do to get a date around here?

I soon realised that if and when I made 'white' matches, they generally fell into one of two categories:

1. The person had an 'exotic' fetish.
2. They swiped right only to let you know that you were cute ... 'for a brown person'.

According to my experiment, the only white match you're likely to get (in South Africa at least) is the one that pairs women of colour with disposability and perpetuates the habitual dumping of these women into the 'throwaway' demographic of what is now a technocratic society. Several studies confirm that Tinder users, especially women of colour, suffer from low self-esteem and reduced body-image satisfaction related to frustration and constant rejection.

Tinder is a pocket, full of rejection. No different from a science-garden experiment on interracial relationships in 1994. Look how far we've come.

# A better life with Bollywood

Friday nights were Bollywood movie nights. It was one of the few nights we were allowed to stay up late, mostly because Bollywood movies are so long that you have to stay up late to finish them. Then we would spend Saturdays mimicking the dances and miming the songs. We dressed up in the lower-quality Indian rags we were allowed to play with, gathered from my mom's cupboard, and put on a show. There's a really embarrassing home video of this somewhere. Let us speak of that no more.

I watched *Veer-Zaara* on a Friday night in 2004, the year of its release. We set up camp in the lounge, made popcorn and settled in for an epic two hours and then some. We were joined by another obligatory presence: a box of silky soft tissues, my mom's trusty companion through her many years of Bollywood movie viewing.

In *Veer-Zaara*, Saamiya Siddiqui meets prisoner number 786 on a gloomy afternoon. Saamiya is a Pakistani lawyer on a mission to pave the way for women's empowerment in the Islamic country. Her late father was a lawyer too, and he believed in the education of girls. He wanted his daughter to have a better life. Now, she has been given prisoner 786's case – her first – after the government decided to review the cases of a few Indians. The odds are stacked against her. The prosecutor is an intimidating, hard-headed patriarch who assures her she is playing a losing game – mostly because she is a woman in a man's world. More than that, prisoner 786 has not spoken a word in twenty-two years and it's unlikely that Saamiya could help him win his freedom without his testimony.

In the early 1980s, Zaara Haayat Khan makes her way to India from Pakistan. In a rare act of rebellion for a woman of that time, she goes against her family's wishes to travel alone and secretly crosses the border with the ashes of her Sikh governess. (Before her passing, the governess had asked Zaara to take her remains to the holy Sikh city of Kiratpur and scatter them in the Sutlej River, among those of her ancestors.) Zaara is the only daughter of a well-known, high-ranking political family in Lahore. She is expected to marry a husband of equal standing to strengthen the position of both families, but cannot see herself conforming to the norms of Pakistani Muslim society. She is far too independent and carefree.

Zaara completes her governess's final rites with the assistance of squadron leader Veer Pratap Singh, who rescues her from a bus accident and takes her the rest of the way. They then embark on a colourful tour of India. The journey ends in Veer's home village where Zaara meets his uncle and aunt who run a school for girls. Veer is an orphan.

He fulfils his final promise of getting her home safely. The anticipation of the train to Lahore is matched by Veer's anxiety. He wants to tell Zaara he loves her. But their moment of eye-locked intimacy is cut short by Zaara's fiancé, who has come looking for her. The train departs fuelled by the gaze of two lovers who will probably never meet again. All Zaara leaves behind is a silver anklet, a stop sign of sorts. A symbol of the end of their bond and a constant reminder that something beautiful ended before it began.

Zaara arrives in Lahore heavy with the baggage of longing. Her feelings for Veer are contradicted by her duty. She has to maintain the family's honour. But a future of furthering her father's political career through marriage to her fiancé feeds her depression and finally a confession haemorrhages out of her. It's blasphemy in a time of religious turmoil between India and Pakistan. It also comes at a time when Pakistan and India are torn apart by terrorism and war.

First she confides in her best friend. Then she confesses to her mother: she has fallen for an Indian man. Zaara's mother curses her, angry at what she sees as disrespect and ignorance on Zaara's part. She warns her daughter that the news of his only child having a relationship with an Indian man will kill her father. Zaara adorns herself with misery during the events leading up to the wedding. Saddened by her disposition, Zaara's best friend writes to Veer and asks him to take her away.

But when Veer arrives in Pakistan, Zaara's mother confronts him in a surprise visit. He is asked to leave. Because he respects elders, he agrees. On his way home, Zaara's jealous fiancé, fluent in corruption and equipped with a tarnished ego, secretly frames him for terrorism and he is imprisoned for life. Zaara is unaware. She never hears from Veer again.

Twenty-two years later, Saamiya, the young lawyer with a point to prove in the name of feminism, meets prisoner 786 in a dark cell. He is nursing a silver anklet in one hand, and his other hand secures a blanket over his shoulders. He is old and his body has been destroyed by heartache. His wrongful conviction has gnawed on him from the inside for far too long. He warms up to

Saamiya after she offers him an Indian sweetmeat similar to the ones his mother used to make him. He agrees to share his story with her on the condition that she never mention Zaara's name in the proceedings or subpoena her family.

In Islam, the number 786 is regarded as a holy number. Saamiya calls Veer 'God's own man'. She promises to restore his identity and return him to India, a land he has not set foot in for twenty-two years.

*Veer-Zaara* has a romantic parallel behind the scenes. The movie is held together by old, untouched compositions by Madan Mohan, an Indian composer who died in the 1970s. His son released the tracks to support the film and requested that Lata Mangeshkar sing the songs as Mohan had asked – another dying wish. Lata is the most respected playback singer in India, with a career spanning seventy years. Her voice can be heard in over a thousand Hindi films, and she sang in over thirty-six regional Indian and foreign languages.

Lata and Madan had a professional relationship that spanned decades. Tying his music to her voice so many years later carries a special kind of poignancy. The partners reunite even after death has parted them. When she arrived in the studio, the legendary singer said, 'I feel I have gone back in past.' The statement echoes Veer's return to his home after twenty-two years.

Bollywood films were where we learnt to make sense of the culture that parts of us unknowingly left behind. They were the vehicles that took us to the homelands of our grandparents and great-grandparents, who arrived in South Africa and never returned. Those vehicles drove our ancestors home, they drove our parents home and, years later, they drove me home.

When I visited India with my mom and sister for the first time a couple of years ago, the warmth of all those Friday movie nights and exposure to my Indian culture left my heart burning with a love for India that seemed bigger than my body could carry. I travelled with an Overseas Citizenship of India passport – documentation you can acquire after a lengthy process of proving you have ancestors from India, some of whom came over as indentured labourers. It was a symbol of belonging. I went to India on an Indian passport; I arrived home with so much more.

But for those who have never visited their country of origin or never again had the chance to return, Bollywood gives them the courage to wear their patriotic hearts on their sleeves. It's the Bollywood movie that lets them escape the existential confusion of being an immigrant. It's the Bollywood movie that stops them, even if just for a couple of hours, from doing as the Romans do, and allows sixteen million people of the Indian diaspora to be consumed by the beating heart of their country as it pounds with yearning through their veins. It provides a connection to their traditions and their roots, and reminds them that while they have left many things behind, they have brought a lot with them as well.

The most decorated song from the *Veer-Zaara* soundtrack is 'Tere Liye', which translates to 'For Your Sake'. It's apposite in meaning. Nothing fits the plight of the diaspora more than the lyrics of the song, which explores the bottling up of emotions. The consequences of living in silence while still holding a candle of hope that things will return to what they once were. All in the name of loyalty and love.

Western societies have long slated Bollywood films for being melodramatic, having thin plots, being repetitive and being far too long. Many people refuse to watch them because they hate reading subtitles and despise the bad sentence construction and grammar when Hindi is translated to English.

But there is a reason for this 'bad' translation: India has a history of maintaining a high rate of illiteracy. This comes as a result of poverty and a lack of access to education. For a long time, literature was incapable of penetrating the populace. Books could not bind people together the same way movies managed to. When the films moved from India to reach the diaspora around the world, the industry was aware of the fact that the people might have lost their home language without speaking it very often, and that English may have been acquired only partially.

Subtitles, therefore, were simplistic, making them easier for people to read. In this way, a viewer on the other end of the world who spoke no Hindi, for example, and only broken English, could still be satisfied because they understood the story. Interestingly, newspaper reading has since increased in India because Bollywood subtitles have helped raise English literacy levels in villages with no access to schools.

Another point of disapproval in the West is the fact that every single Bollywood film is a musical. They can't understand it. They find it irritating and unnecessary.

An extensive original soundtrack of anything between five and fourteen songs supports each Bollywood film. The actors don't sing them; they mime. Behind the scenes, a team of composers, musical directors, session musicians and playback singers is hard at work.

The only two things more important to Bollywood than the music are happy endings and showing respect for mothers in every single storyline. Bollywood respects mothers the way the offspring of Indian families enjoy Hindi films. They have to. They have to love them like they love their maternal guardians. They. Just. Have. To. And like our mothers, Bollywood (to an extent) helps shape our hearts and minds. First it sets up the battle between the emotional and the rational, and then the films extinguish the fight between what is kitsch and all that defies common sense with a well of victory: victory for the lovers, the fighters, the abolished. You can't escape its triumph and the sense of winning that the last scene of every movie gifts you.

Bollywood lives in the Mumbai of our hearts. A place of the striving. A place of the abandoned. A place of conflict between moral and immoral choices. It is the lost-and-found bin of emotions and it houses our love. And it quite literally sings us through the streets of our feelings.

In all fairness, though, Bollywood suffers the same level of success – or failure, rather – as Hollywood when it comes to quality. Three-quarters of the releases are nonsense, the remainder quite good. But the West's denigration of Bollywood is much harsher when compared to its US counterpart. For some reason, people can't seem to step away from insulting the Indian film industry's plots even though they are as far-fetched and fanciful as Broadway musicals (whose plots are never deemed thin). I have never once heard a white person say a bad word about *Grease*, for example, and is this not also a blockbuster where songs pop up at any given moment? What difference does it make if this same thing occurs in another language born of a different country?

Finally, there's this age-old argument: Bollywood movies are stupid because the lovers never kiss and they're always coy and run around trees and stuff. This is what *we* call culture. India is a conservative country and the film industry has to reflect this because it plays to a vast audience who possess a variety of ethical views. In newer films, physical romantic interaction has become the norm, but not without tussles between the producers and the Central Board of Film Certification. Often, films are cut and censored to avoid the social scrutiny and criticism of culturally taboo issues like public displays of affection. Some viewers don't mind an onscreen kiss, but others find it offensive and culturally inappropriate. I believe in a free and fair media. Censorship is generally wrong, but what if, in the case of Bollywood, the censorship of physical intimacy is right? After all, art imitates life and all that. People never kiss in public in India. They're modest, and modesty is honour and respect. Even *Veer-Zaara* only sees the hero and heroine touch each other in a fantasy song sequence.

Maybe it's this kind of censorship that keeps Bollywood films housed in a cloud of warmth and innocence. In this way, they remain wholesome. People crave this. Hollywood, on the other hand, breeds ambivalence. There is always an air of indifference when it comes to family, for example. Bollywood does the opposite. The stories unfold in a utopia of pre-cynicism where there is faith in love and patriotism and parents.

And as much as these movies are castigated in foreign societies, so too are they embraced. Bollywood isn't a billion-dollar industry that puts Hollywood in the shade only because of its home country and the Indian diaspora. These films have penetrated the globe in ways we forget to mention. The Soviet Union (at the time) started to screen Hindi films as far back as the 1950s. The industry has an – almost inexplicable – mass following in Haiti and the Dominican Republic. The films come in peace to both the Israelis and the Palestinians. Their thin storylines are translated into dozens of languages from French to Mandarin and beyond.

Virtue is nourishing, regardless of where you're from. Citizens carry the lyrics of Bollywood songs around the globe – even if they have to recite them in English. Every country in the world speaks the language of love just like every country in the world understands the language of grief. Familiar feelings are family and so Bollywood movies are accepted in the homes of many. The over-the-top acting and plots are forgiven because of the innocence that is their bedrock. Bollywood is good people. And often, Bollywood is life.

Life is explosively colourful and the characters are explosively colourful. The films are materially and fundamentally vibrant. The clothing is rich with the tapestry of the culture and the people are rich with the personalities we've all encountered at some point in our lives: those who have loved you and those who have left you. The enemy, the friend, the teacher, the villain, the lover.

Life is repetitive and Bollywood movies are repetitive. Repetition doesn't always cause boredom. Sometimes it's just structure, and structure is control. Sometimes repetition is trust. We wake up, go to work, go to sleep, and in between all of that we do other things, like eat. This pattern of behaviour is as old as, well, India, and in some ways it's endearing – just like those movies. The more things change, the more they stay the same.

Bollywood is a song and dance. Life … should be. We often live without singing and dancing for periods of time, but we can't live without it at all. Just like a Bollywood movie, life would be incomplete without these two things. It would lack joy and celebration. What would we do at weddings or birthday parties? How would we enter a New Year? Reality TV would suffer without singing and dancing shows, I'll tell you that much. Music is memory and without it there would hardly be anything to recall. Our lives have a soundtrack, just like Bollywood movies.

Life is long and the films are long: like the script of any Hindi film, life too can transport you from one emotional town to the next. There's drama and comedy and tragedy, and it's all wrapped up in one lengthy package. Moments of emotional investment are contrasted with feelings of wanting to give in and give up. There's a time for loyalty and a time for betrayal. And sometimes it feels like these things go on forever.

In *Veer–Zaara*, the prosecution opens with a pretty solid case. The twenty-two-year-old fabricated evidence has managed to stand firm in what is supposed to be a democratic Pakistan. Saamiya can taste loss. Her tongue is tied with hopelessness. She puts on shoes of desperation and, without Veer's knowledge, travels to India in search of someone who can prove prisoner 786's true identity. She runs into a dead end. Veer's aunt and uncle died many years ago. But then…

At the girls' school in Veer's village she finds Zaara, who fled to India after she was told that Veer died on his way home. She lives in his house. She runs his family's school. And she goes back to Pakistan one last time, to clear his name.

The movie ends with Veer and Zaara bidding farewell to Saamiya at the Wagah border crossing in Pakistan. Veer kneels when he steps over it and greets the sand of his homeland with his hand, holding on to each grain as though he will never let go again. Then he takes Zaara's hand and they return to their village together. A victory in more ways than one.

And this is where Bollywood leaves life behind and the paths of fact and fiction disconnect.

Bollywood movies always have a happy ending. Closure is a trademark that features in every single story. A definite end is compulsory. Life only has a definite end in death, but if it must close – and it must – then let it close with this: eventually, love wins.

# The curious case of
# the old white architect

All systemic racism gets its way eventually. It's hard to believe, but it's true. It's not as perverse as it once was. It doesn't stare you blankly in the face, look you up and down, and spit at your feet. But it's there, at the frontlines. Winning. All the time.

It's in the little manual that companies release every year to prove they have met their equal opportunities numbers. It's in the questions and answers that turn the brown heads filling office space into little beads on an abacus. Rattling around while white corporates, who still own the majority of capital in the country, shuffle and shake their standing in order to 'balance' the scales. *How many black (in the constitutional definition) people do we employ? Where do we need changes so we can check those boxes? How can we manipulate these numbers in the boardroom when management sits down so that the round table looks equal?*

The doors of the institutions that hire us are still made of misery. The turnstiles at the entrances are fuelled by systemic racism, and every time we pass through, our legs turn to jelly. The imbalance in our strides is intensified by a persistent historical power.

The power of white-owned media organisations, for example,

still has a hold over me. The power of systemic racism is dark magic. The institutions themselves are a horcrux. Their magic is so powerful, so supreme, so 'whitely supreme' that these organisations house portions of the souls they steal in order to remain immortal. Or that's at least what it feels like to me. A piece of my soul still resides there.

I spent a year at a popular weekly magazine, and I spent about three trying to forget the memories of that place. I clawed at sanity and tried to maintain some degree of enthusiasm for the craft of journalism. I spent a lot of time convincing myself that working in media would not always be a slow death, a prolonged suicide of my mind and a continuous existential crisis.

Working there made me world-weary. It sewed my opinion of the media into a blanket that muffled my ambition: the media was a dog show and people of colour would always be the mutts. Panting after white editors to get a byline bone thrown at them or sitting in corners, punished because they refused to submit. Untrainable cage dogs. I fell into the latter category.

Now, I will happily, proudly even, admit that I am untrainable. I am rebellious in the face of authority, I do not like being told what to do by people dumber than I am – as a life rule – and I am oiled by way too much independent thinking to be a yes-woman. This I will fight to the death for: I am not a freakin' abacus bead. I am not a head to be counted and forgotten. Sometimes the bead in me rears its monstrous, worn face, but I am getting better at slapping it from my thoughts. I am *not* a bead. I'm sure of that now. And I get more sure every day.

But in 2012 I was not sure at all and my place in the world made no sense to me. When I finished my honours in journalism at Stellenbosch in 2011, I entered a competition run by a major media house. The winner received a fairly good cash prize and a year's paid internship at one of their magazines.

Journalism students from all over the country entered, and quite a few were from my class. There was supposed to be one winner, but three white Afrikaans students joined me as winners. I was the only one who got the money – in exchange for fewer bylines than the rest of the winners, as it turned out.

The first thing that entered my mind was the numbers game I spoke about before. I questioned my skills: Should I not have won? Was I only there to maintain a good BEE demographic while keeping the place appropriately white? Was I the box they would tick on the employment-equity form? Was I just a statistic while the other three were the pillars of institutional perpetuation?

Do you know what this feels like? These thoughts? They feel like possession. They feel like strangulation. They feel like panic and pain. And they feel as though they will only go away if you make yourself small or disappear.

There is a special kind of self-doubt that blossoms from systemic racism, and the present and post-traumatic effects of it are completely unafraid. These effects express themselves wilfully, and they are both predictable and erratic. They steal any semblance of common sense from the mind that suffers them.

The terrifying narrative of systemic inequality is disseminated with such conviction. It concusses its victims, whose speech is broken and words forgotten. It instils feverish thoughts that cry with desperation. *Let me out of this infection, let me believe in myself, what is happening?* it screams. This existential crisis felt like it would kill me. When it passes through me now and then, I remember that feeling well. It made me feel like an actor cast in a horror movie I didn't audition for. The set had no refuge. No stairs. Nowhere for me to go.

143

Before we started working at the magazines, the editors and news editors arranged a meeting with the four winners. They came through to Stellenbosch and while we waited outside a pub for them, one of the Afrikaans students started a conversation about which magazines we would be placed at. He suggested that the white-targeted magazines were perfect fits for the three of them, because they were white and would not be seen dead at a magazine catering for another demographic.

Then this kid politely turned to me and said: 'You, of course, will be going to [a magazine aimed at black readers].' I don't think I need to explain the ignorance and racism here. His polite disposition quickly shifted into a massive side-eye. I could have smacked the white off him. Obviously, I did not. I inhaled my words. And even though those words were contemplations of my own construction, they were poisonous and unkind to me.

I could have smacked the white off the same student earlier in the year when we visited the Apartheid Museum in Johannesburg. He pointedly said that I would have been okay during apartheid because I would have passed the pencil test. He pretended this was a compliment, ignorant of the fact that it was anything but.

This kind of casual racism is worse than the in-your-face kind. To me, it's worse than expressing open hostility because it displays a kind of cold ambivalence so deeply entrenched in the offender it's sickening. Casual racism is an over-performer. That might seem like a contradiction. It is not. Casual racism shows; it doesn't tell.

Don't get me wrong – horrifying acts of racist violence carried out by regimes or terrorist groups are maddening and incomprehensible. These incidents are not rare, but they are hard to answer for. The meaning of these tragedies is so useless. People's lives taken for what? Why would people *behave* this way? The easy answer is hate. And these acts of hate are punishable.

The casual racist, however, almost always gets away with their words because they do not warrant the punishment demanded by racism that is regarded as more hostile and dominant. But casual racism is the act of manipulative dominance. Its communication displays a calculated kind of cunning. It is often delivered to the person of colour as some kind of backhanded compliment, but it is the thief of our joy and that is exactly what it intends to be.

The reason I entered the competition was because I desperately wanted to stay in Cape Town. There was no way I was going back to Pretoria; I hated it there. But I needed money to stay and the prize would be a massive help. I had spent the five-year retirement annuity I earned at my previous teaching job on a post-grad degree in journalism, and my once lekker bank balance had landed close to nothing.

I also entered because working at one of the biggest magazines in South Africa would bring with it excellent industry experience. There was a lot to learn. I found out later that I would only learn how to become a gold-medallist at crying myself to sleep every night because of hardcore prejudice. I went from zero to caged dog real quick, and in that cage I became a hard-ass.

The other interns all got to go out on boss stories. Well, not really boss. But they were doing real journalism. I got to write thirty-word DVD reviews, thirty-word app reviews and the occasional CD review. The dude who edited this portion of the magazine was one of the nicest people in the building, though, so I didn't mind working with him.

Then, of course, I was assigned the odd interview that happened in a township like Epping or Philippi. The brown person covering the brown stories, so to speak. Again, I didn't mind, but the prejudice in assigning these stories to me was obvious. Also, most of them didn't get published. I'd do the story, submit and then have the editor shout 'What *kak* is this?' from across the newsroom. There were also a lot of *'foks'* and *'fok* Hajis' thrown into the mix. There was no reason for the scolding, in my opinion. I won the damn competition; I could obviously write well. Or nah? I didn't know. Existential tortures, remember?

Systemic racists have slight or no regard for people and communities that do not fulfil their vision of the world. There is no need for a moral responsibility. Even if it's not obvious, there is a disregard for people other than their own, and this disregard is powered by contempt and hatred. In white-owned media organisations, people of colour only exist to be antagonised. We are constantly engaged in battles and acts of petty sabotage: struggles for more opportunities, equal pay and the fight to be heard and respected. We receive little encouragement and mentorship. No effort is made to display any semblance of pleasure in working with us. Instead, the only efforts made are to convey disapproval.

I often got shouted at because of my politics. Like the time I was told to write a story about a black youth who spoke at a TEDx event. I was broken when I was told the story was not good enough simply because I refused to change the details of his life to something more stereotypically pleasing.

The truth: he was an intelligent, well-rounded teenager who came from an impoverished but stable home with a healthy family dynamic. He offered mentoring and maths tutoring to the rest of the matriculants at his school.

The magazine wanted me to make his story more *Tsotsi*-like. It was demanded that I change the details of his life to say he was involved in gangs and drugs before he changed for the better.

*What the actual fuck?*

I fought hard for this guy in the most polite way possible. I was even apologetic, but I lost. They changed the story anyway. I demanded that my byline be removed. It was. Losing one brown byline is a small price to pay for the perpetuation of stereotypes. The obvious reason for the editorial manipulation was that no one wanted a story of a good black kid. Only white kids are intrinsically exceptional.

The newsroom in this kind of organisation is the reality that counters the rainbow-nation magic offered by advertising. Companies like these are not the shiny space we're offered in pay-off lines where people of colour have meaning in their lives outside of the struggles they face. The stories happening inside newsrooms like these are different from the ones we read on the outside. The stories we live on the inside are different from the ones we are expected to tell.

One day, I got summoned to the front desk to chat to a retired architect who wanted to speak to a journalist about a possible story. He had no appointment. What he had was a lot of time and a healthy bout of racism.

When you're a person of colour interning at an extremely white organisation, an 'order' like this can be translated as such: everyone else, including the other (white) interns, is far too important and busy with actual stuff; send the skivvy down to waste her time with one of the hundreds of people who think they have a scoop for the magazine. It gets her out the way and gives our eyes a rest from the constant effort of ignoring her.

I'm sure other interns have to do this kind of thing all the time, realistically. But it's hard not to take the above stance when you're literally the only one doing it while everyone else is getting their story ideas accepted in the news meetings and yours are being overlooked.

People popped in uninvited for lengthy story briefs all the time. Me having to go talk to them happened all the time too. Eventually, I trained myself to enjoy it. It gave me a lot of insight into the madness of the world, and it was a free pass out of a depressing and scary office.

Once, someone's mother-in-law came in to see me. Well, not me specifically. But there I was. She was trying to get her son's money back from his ex-wife. As her story went on, I realised there was no money. She was referring to the financial contribution he made to their marriage. Like for food and stuff. 'She ate all the food he bought her. We want that money back. She needs to be exposed,' were this woman's actual words. What a wonderful waste of time. A healthy hour out of the office and absolutely no need to write a bunch of crap.

There was a white belly-dancing instructor who tried to convince me to investigate the Turkish man she had married. It would be a massive exposé, she said. She fell in love with him and then discovered he just wanted citizenship. He now paid her no attention at all and she realised he didn't really love her. She needed the story because she needed closure. Again, a wonderful waste of my time.

But the most memorable of these 'I've got a story for you' experiences was the one I had with the retired architect. He had a sense of entitlement taller than the building I worked in. His was a story I should have demanded I be allowed to write. His was a story that the magazine should have published because it provided an education in the workings of a white mind in a democratic South Africa. It was excellent proof of the ignorance and pride of the delusional racist who – with a sense of conviction firmer than a marble floor – claims to not be racist at all.

He was thoroughly displeased to see me. He wanted to know

exactly who I was and what I did at the magazine. Was I the receptionist or someone's assistant? He wanted to know why the editor did not come and chat to him herself. Then he dropped the 'W' word: 'When I saw you I was so confused. I thought you would be white.' I smiled through my teeth, bit down hard and turned my molars into sawdust. I responded with a cappuccino, on me. God knows I needed one to wash down all my finely ground teeth.

With milk-foam-framed lips plumped up by false teeth, he proceeded to lean in and tell me what he claimed was a state secret.

'I know exactly why taxi drivers are responsible for most of the motor accidents in South Africa,' he said.

Oh, this is going to be good, I thought. I know what you think he said; you think he said: because they're black. Nope. The story took a turn I could never in my wildest dreams have imagined.

He went with the whole 'I'm an extremely culturally aware South African' angle: 'You see, it's because in the black culture, when babies are young, the mothers carry them on their backs so their eyesight never develops. It happens with the girl babies as well.'

Whew, what a relief he mentioned the girl babies, I thought. If he'd been racist, a self-proclaimed liberal *and* a sexist, that would have been too much.

'But of course,' he continued, 'it's only black men that drive taxis and because they have undeveloped eyes, they cause all the accidents.'

Wow. His point was that there was a massive problem with black culture, with how black women raised their children. They were creating road-killers because they did not know better. He thought he was sympathetic in his over-performance. But really, he was indifferent, cold, ignorant and racist. He wanted me to write the story so that he, a privileged white architect who unjustly made his money during apartheid and had little else to do now besides rationalise white superiority, could share his thinking with the rest of South Africa. Because the white reality is the right reality and it needs to be manifested in all parts of society – including those pertaining to taxi drivers.

There was no better metaphor than this man for the newsroom in which I worked. A racist assumption bred from a mind made by systemic racism.

This man was the walking, talking racist ideology of that office. Of so many offices. And like those offices, he comprised a mass of ideas and assumptions. A worldview like a tumour that belonged to a group of people whose beliefs continue to spread the disease that is systemic racism. A disease that uses the lens of white superiority to interpret both physiology and culture. A disease that maintains the constructive image of whiteness, and the destructive image of people of colour.

This specific experience at this specific job remains significant to me. It is a reminder of the epidemic that perpetuates stereotypes and prejudices and popular beliefs – when it comes to young black boys who live in townships, for example.

This specific experience at this specific job is as clear an example as any that as long as this kind of racism exists, it will continue to inform the actions of those in power. Those actions will continue to foster this kind of racism, and this kind of racism will continue to foster that special kind of ignorance that makes the racist incapable of recognising their racist ways. And like this, the terrifying narrative of systemic inequality will continue to be disseminated, concussing its victims.

I survived this concussion the hard way and I am learning that no system is worth me forgetting my words. No system will break my speech. And I will remain unapologetic about that.

# When Nelson Mandela died

When Nelson Mandela died, I had one job: take pictures and tweet about it. I was so grateful. You see, I am a faulty journalist. I like writing, but I don't like reporting. My wiring is messed up and the electricity doesn't always spark. I am not interested in chasing breaking news. I don't believe in scoops. I have no desire to be on the scene, doorstopping people for interviews and comment so that I can win the journalist Olympics. The idea of making phone calls so I can write lengthy investigative stories that ensure my byline lands up on the front page is of absolutely no interest to me.

So when Madiba passed on and I was still social media editor at the *Mail & Guardian* (*M&G*), I felt like the most blessed human being in the world. Many journalists will point and laugh at me for thinking any of this, but to me, it was a gift. A gift wrapped in honour and humility. A gift with zero need to rat-race with other journalists. This was the stuff digital journalism was made of. Accessible and immediate information, filled with emotion for people on the ground who couldn't be as close to the events as I was. And all this was possible via one click on a mobile phone. This was my forte.

When Nelson Mandela died, his death had already been written. His obituaries were composed months before he took his last breath. They rested in the secure and secret hard drives of editors. Special editions were planned and ready to be pressed. Images were sourced and purchased in high-res from reputable photo wires months in advance. Shorter, punchier pieces with 'did you know' trivia were prepped. They would support the lengthier articles containing the finer details. At the *M&G*, all the digital content was queued and ready to be posted on every platform possible. Listicles, gifs, memes, videos, slide-shows. All of them. They lay waiting on the back-end benches of a special microsite that would go live as soon as news broke. Extra servers across the ocean hummed with enthusiasm, ready to host more page views. All hands were on deck, each individual finger fulfilling some role in a carefully planned granular strategy.

The only thing missing in all of this, of course, was a date. What year, month and day would host this content? When would the announcement of his passing be made? We waited with breath that was bated and feet that tapped and thumbs that twiddled, until 5 December 2013.

This is a sad confession and a terrible journalistic truth that does nothing to eradicate the vulture stereotype of the media. We are disgusting scavengers who wait to feed off the suffering of others and, often, of each other as well. But it is also a fair reflection of how seriously we took the imminent loss of the first democratically elected president of South Africa. His life deserved to be lauded with material composed in the sweat of pure effort and dedication. More than that, journalists were tasked with quenching the thirst of an entire nation who wanted to drink from his life a little longer. In death, stories are cathartic.

Information is the bridge between loss and acceptance. Social media becomes web therapy.

When Nelson Mandela died, I had just returned from a holiday in India. I came back with a Goa tan, a Delhi belly (not the sick kind, the fat kind, from eating way too much naan bread and delicious food with clarified butter) and Japanese encephalitis. I went straight to work. I had no inkling of the weird virus living in my body. My aching bones, migraine and constant fever were jet lag, I was convinced, and I didn't care about that. I don't really believe in jet lag.

I arrived at the office in a hoodie that had not been washed in over three weeks. Do you know what India smells like? It smells like human faeces and old ash and life, real life. It is the most amazing place in the world. I brought that amazing place with me that day and wore it wherever I went. It was rainy and I had no choice. There were bigger priorities than going home to change and smell better. Things needed doing. Queue-standing, for example, was of absolute importance. There were identification queues, verification queues and accreditation queues. After all that, we received our passes to the statesman's funeral, memorial service and other newsworthy events. If you were one of the people standing within a 500-metre radius of me that day, you also got a free tour of the great subcontinent through your nasal passages. I hope you enjoyed the ride.

Mourning had started a few months prior to Mandela's death. In June 2013, he was hospitalised in Pretoria. It wasn't long before #prayforMadiba started trending on Twitter. I started an *M&G* Instagram account, so along with tweeting about absolutely everything, I also posted pictures of absolutely everything. President Jacob Zuma cancelled a trip to Mozambique so he could visit Madiba. Tweeted. Schoolchildren in uniform dropped by in their hundreds to deliver cards and gifts and flowers. Instagrammed. Catholic nuns lit candles. Instagrammed.

Outside the hospital, there were lots and lots of cameras. I had never before covered a news story surrounded by celebrity journalists from CNN and the BBC and Al-Jazeera and Sky. Any news outlet you could think of was there. No one from my generation had seen anything this huge happen, and if they couldn't be there, then I was. I made memes and gifs, and I shared the stories of stories of everyone who pitched up and had something to say and something to share. Like the ninety-year-old woman who had been an ANC supporter her whole life and forced the nurses to drag her from her hospital bed so she could pay her respects with the crowd outside. For anything more hard-hitting and 'journalistic', the public could watch Al-Jazeera or CNN or the BBC or Sky. Or the work of all the other South African journalists who were doing an excellent job reporting. There were balloons and banners and teddy bears. Tweeted and Instagrammed.

ANC vigils sporadically took place before and after his death. For example, they bussed in heaps of people to the areas surrounding the hospital in Pretoria that June. They marched and sang and prayed. Soon after, when they were done with Madiba, they used the opportunity to picket and campaign for Jacob Zuma's presidency for the next few hours. It wasn't long before #prayforMadiba turned into #prayforanotherterm.

I experienced what can only be described as an emotional landslide. Initially, I felt on top of the world, inspired by the party that fought for our freedom. I remember feeling moved by their pride as they took to the streets. I remember feeling bleak for them about their imminent loss. A decades-long personal relationship with a hero of freedom who was about to leave them.

Those feelings quickly devolved into deep sorrow. Huge trucks pulled up and unfolded into podiums. Disturbingly large sound systems called for the support of Zuma. Yellow T-shirts emblazoned with ANC propaganda in support of the president were fed to the masses. I remember feeling like each was a betrayal. These offensive gestures continued. Tied together by disrespect, they hung like a banner at the foot of a stalwart's hospital bed.

When Nelson Mandela died, there was a massive memorial service at the FNB Stadium in Johannesburg. The Calabash was at capacity. Love and mourning erupted from every seat. Madiba's dream nation shook its rattle for him one last time in a rainbow arena. It was rainy and it was cold. Journalists met outside the SABC offices in Auckland Park. The government arranged for us to be bussed in at the crack of dawn. We arrived before the crowds got in, frazzled and unprepared for the rain. We gathered in the pressroom where we were treated to black plastic bags for raincoats and had access to all the plug sockets our hearts desired. Computers and phones needed constant charging. Live blogs and social media feeds needed updating. Missing a single detail because of a flat battery was a bigger failure than I could handle that day.

My heart stirred when a hundred thousand people sang the national anthem together. The stadium roared with passion. When they sang 'Senzenina', my heart stirred some more. Then Baleka Mbete took the microphone to address the crowd and, with her slow rendition of the same song, my heart stopped stirring. She did not have a great voice. I lolled hard.

FNB Stadium has a basement parking lot with a 'secret' entrance where the celebrities and dignitaries enter so they can be taken straight to their seats on the stage. If you had a special pass, you were allowed to hang out there. The photographers possessed these gems. They snapped until their camera triggers were filed down. I had somehow managed to convince someone that Instagram photography was a real thing, so I was down there too.

I remember thinking, *Gosh, I really must educate myself on the leaders of African countries.* I knew none of them when they entered that foyer. Learning their names is still on my bucket list. There was no time for Google, so I ashamedly avoided tweeting pictures of them. How would I caption them? 'African leader 1'? 'African leader 2'? *God, I am awful,* I thought. I was comforted by the fact that most of the journalists around me were muttering to each other and asking who the African dignitaries were as well. But this comfort did not eradicate my shame.

The leaders and celebrities from the West? Now those I knew. They were the ones in the history books and the news. Of course I knew them. The prince of Monaco and his South African wife (she did not look happy, and I don't think it was because of Madiba). Bono. The Obamas. Click, click. Snap, snap.

Then, all at once, there was silence. Heads bowed. Cameras continued clicking, but it was as though they suddenly came with a mute button. Ma Winnie entered. She came in like a vision. A graceful, regal vision. Her frame made taller by her power and her legend. Her eyes downcast, her body clothed in black. A daughter on each arm. She walked in the centre and slightly ahead of them. I remember feeling like that moment passed slowly and quickly at the same time. What stature. All current ANC members looked like fools in comparison. Court jesters, I'm afraid. The magnitude of Winnie Madikizela-Mandela remains, to this day, indescribable to me. I still get goosebumps thinking about it. I also get incredibly sad about the fight she won for a nation that mostly forgot about her.

When Nelson Mandela died, I thought about my ethics and African studies lecturer a lot. Dr Simphiwe Sesanti walked into our journalism class one day filled with robustness and rage. I got the distinct impression he was tired of how the white students revered Nelson Mandela. He was offended (and rightly so) by the fact that it was becoming clearer with each lecture that Mandela was just about the only black South African they recognised and respected. The only black South African they were ever likely to reference with any degree of positivity. So, with vigour, he shouted, 'Nelson Mandela did not free us! We freed Nelson!'

Denial screamed from the throats of the privileged students who got the best deal. They fought back with 'buts'. There were also gasps and murmurs. My friend Sarah and I turned to each other, mouths open and eyes wide. We had one mutual thought: blasphemy. Sesanti, almost bouncing off the walls, fists in the air, gave us a lesson in apartheid warfare. In the brutalities of frontlines and the dangers of being outside the prison walls for twenty-seven years instead of behind them.

Aware of the outcry in the classroom but unafraid, he repeated his war cry a little louder: 'Nelson Mandela did not free us! We freed Nelson!' That was in 2011. It's taken seven years, but today, I believe him. Nelson Mandela did not free us.

# Joining a cult is a terrible idea

When I married Rebecca, I ordered a wedding dress off the internet. It looked kind of awesome and I paid just over R600 for it. A bargain for a wedding dress. Some people pay the equivalent of a down payment on a small house. The postage cost me about another R200. Still a bargain.

When it arrived, I realised why it was so cheap. It appeared to be an old man's hanky stretched and stitched into some kind of curtain. There was no old-man snot, but there were a lot of loose beads that fell from it like a breadcrumb trail as soon as I unpacked the … thing. Awesome it was not.

I was angry. I went back to the drawing board that is the internet. Not to look for another dress. Oh no. I went in search of reviews of this posh place in London with the awesome discounted dresses. Every single review I read, including the ones right there on the website, which I hadn't bothered to look at before, said the store was a complete sham.

Most of the comments went like this:

'This place is not based in London. Don't fall for it.'

'Save your money.'

'What a rip off!'

'This place never delivers and when they do deliver, the dresses are just disappointing.'

'These dresses are sewn by underpaid, blind Cambodian children. You are supporting child slavery.' (Okay, that last one is a lie. No one said that. But the item I received certainly looked that way.)

When I was done reading, I facepalmed myself so hard, the indentation is still imprinted on my hand. Everyone told me the same thing and they were right. I *should* have done my research. Duh! What is wrong with me? You would think that I'd have learnt my lesson and not paid a lot of money for overblown promises. You would think that I'd have learnt my lesson in 2009, when I paid R3500 for a five-day workshop with what, in my view, is a cult.

I only only came to the conclusion that it was a cult when the trauma ended and my research began. A cult is a social group that subscribes to certain religious, philosophical or spiritual beliefs. What makes a cult a cult, is that followers offer devotion to an unorthodox leader through a process of indoctrination. Historically, cults were associated only with religion. Their leaders and followers were the rebellious offspring of more popular religions.

Cults remain in the realm of contention and controversy in pop culture, religion, academia and social studies. Their indoctrination can take the shape of abuse, coercive persuasion, humiliation, hypnosis and brainwashing. The workshop I did at the Insight Training Centre of Light in Johannesburg met all of these criteria. It may have met them unconventionally, but meet them it did.

At the time of my joining – or rather, participation – I was going through some stuff. I saw a lot of quack therapists who didn't really know what they were doing, my life was a mess and

I was desperate. I was the kind of desperate that makes a kid steal from their own family to buy tik. The only difference was that I needed a high from life. I wanted to *like* life. I wanted to enjoy it. I wanted to be life's addict. You can't steal joy from anyone, unfortunately, but this secluded little place on a large property in Fourways promised that, in just five days, they would hand me joy on a silver platter.

Joy or death? It felt like those were my only choices. I paid the deposit and went to Turning Point.

Turning Point is torture. It *promises* to radically change the direction of the participant's life so they can exist in the world differently and have a better understanding of their behaviour by being aware of the role consciousness plays in their lives. But Turning Point is not this. It. Is. Torture.

Turning Point promised I would learn a 'new way of being'. Well, let me tell you, when I was done, I definitely bee'd [*sic*] in a new way. I bee'd like a person who just got the biggest shock of their life. I had allowed myself to be tortured and humiliated and subjugated by a cult. Nothing teaches you how to enjoy life on the other side more than having the life sucked out of you inside a temple of doom and gloom by a wealthy pop-prophet who pours psychobabble and profanity into your ear over a loudspeaker.

Turning Point should not be called Turning Point. It should be called 'The sharp corner you take before you break yourself in half and enter hell'.

I only read what people had to say about Turning Point and the other courses at the Insight Training Centre about three years after that five-day workshop in the summer of 2009. I was too afraid of what I would learn. I also carried around a lot of guilt for being quiet about it for so long. As a journalist, I should have written something ages ago. I should have gone back to do the second workshop – as a graduate of the first – and blown the lid off the whole thing. I didn't. I'm writing about it now, though, so that's something, I guess.

If you don't read past this point, take this one thing away with you: never, ever, ever participate in Turning Point or any of the other workshops at the Insight Training Centre of Light (which you can only pay to participate in, by the way, once you have completed Turning Point – the first phase). Never ever, *ever* set foot in the Insight Training Centre in Fourways, *ever*. And if you do, take Derek Watts or whoever is doing *Carte Blanche* these days with you. In fact, take Debora Patta. Debora Patta doesn't shoot blanks.

The training centre's website offers this definition of the Turning Point workshop: 'It represents an intensive period in human life, with fifty hours of concentrated self-reflection, intro-spection and exploration of profound possibilities.' When they talk about an 'intensive period in human life', they aren't messing around.

I started Turning Point on a Wednesday. I can't remember what month it was, but it was warm. First, we had to register by handing in a compulsory questionnaire. It was confidential and required a number of invasive and very personal answers to questions of the same nature. We were warned that if we did not approach these questions with blatant honesty and the utmost degree of vulnerability, no point in our lives would be turned. I wanted all the points of my life to turn hard, so I answered the tough questions with a lot of tough truths. After registration, we entered the hall.

We were a group of about fifty. When we reached our seats, the entire room flooded with the theme song from *2001: A Space*

*Odyssey*. It blared through the sound system. I don't know how they knew we were in our 'positions'. Someone was obviously watching us. As the music crescendoed, pop-prophet Royee Banai entered the hall. We only ever sat when he ordered us to do so. If we sat before his command, he shouted at us.

This same process was adhered to at the start of every session, but after that first night, the procedure had a little addition: when the music played, we were ordered to raise our hands slowly towards the sky with our eyes closed and, as the notes ascended, we were to stretch up as if we were high-fiving god.

The first session started at 6 p.m. Once we walked in and a few hours had passed, we had no sense of time. It was taken from us. No clocks hung from the walls and the front desk always kept our watches and phones before we began. Anyone who did not follow this protocol got thrown out. Oh, and shouted at. The name of the game was humiliation, and it was only when you exited and the session ended that you realised it was 3 a.m. During that time, we did not eat and we did not sleep and there were four days left to go. There were four days with Royee Banai left to go.

When you grow up in a culture where mental illness is not recognised, the secret of your disease eats away at you more than the disease itself. That's exactly what I felt like at that point in my life. There were few places I could turn to. I was told several times to pray myself out of it. In this way, among others, religion is a cult as well. It is a system that shuns anyone or anything that challenges its claims to truth. In many cultures and religions – including my own – mental illness is not a truth. It cannot exist if your faith does. This is no different from coercing people the way lost prophets do in actual cults.

It's kind of funny: a lot of people enter cults because they find religion and the norms of society too restrictive and they're scared of feeling alienated. In their search for something better, they end up being a part of something just as restrictive and potentially alienating for a whole host of other reasons.

The threat of being alienated from my culture by my personal demons left me with two options:

1. Allow myself to be coerced into praying away those demons.
2. Keep the demons a secret and pretend to be coerced into a certain way of thinking regardless.

I went with option two for a long time. But then, my demons became so life-threatening that I signed up for a workshop that promised to help me out.

A desperate, broken human will do and believe anything that promises to make them feel better. I needed to feel better. Besides, it was easy to publicly announce my forthcoming participation at Turning Point because the course was about 'making better decisions in life'. I could frame it as a professional investment instead of the therapy I needed for my mental breakdown.

Now. Let me tell you about Royee Banai.

Royee Banai was our trainer for the duration of the course. His bio on the website today says: 'For the last 20 years Royee Banai has been involved in the sphere of Personal Transformation, facilitating self-development and self-discovery workshops at the Insight Training Centre with well over 10 000 individuals since the year 2000 at the Centre of Light, situated 9km from Fourways.'

During our lengthy sessions with Royee, he could not stop telling us about his own transformation as a selling point. We needed to trust him because his life was awesome. He told us that it was because he operated on a different plane of consciousness and behaviour that he was a top martial-arts competitor who received eight distinctions in matric with a pass mark of 97.67 per cent and two degrees – an undergrad and honours degree in psychology. This information formed part of his more 'friendly' soliloquies. Other themes that featured in the short, heart-warming and inspirational portions of his motivational talks were aspects like money and love.

Royee Banai did not need money, apparently, because he knew how to love. He knew how to love everyone. He operated above the plane of money and so love fed him. One night during a short break, however, I took a walk through the massive prop-erty, wandered too far from the main building and into a field, and saw a bunch of high-end German cars parked on one of the unoccupied portions of land. Big German cars have big German boots. Was that where they kept the money we paid them to tell us that money and material things don't matter?

Royee Banai's multiple accomplishments in martial arts had come in handy one night when he apparently physically attacked one of the Turning Point participants. In 2014, a woman called Ntoli phoned into Radio 702 during an interview with Royee Banai to tell listeners about the assault. At the time of the broad-cast, Ntoli was just over fifty years old. When she'd done the workshop, she stood up during the session where Royee and his minions force people to kneel down and pound pillows on the floor in anger. This pounding went on for about an hour, she said. I have a bad grasp of time and can't really confirm the duration, but when I did it, it definitely felt like an exceptionally long period of screaming and pillow beating.

When Ntoli rose to her feet in the middle of this drill, she said, Royee slapped her face. She fell back and he proceeded to kick her while she was down and force her back into the kneeling position.

Displaying fear or incompetence is frowned upon in that place. According to the teaching, fear is a state of unawareness of the conscious mind and is not to be obeyed. Reacting to fear is considered a weakness and treated with aggression, humiliation and punishment. Over and above that, no one is allowed to ask another participant if they are okay when these things happen. That is a weakness in itself and all Turners – so to speak – must rise above it. All physical attacks are therefore justified according to the Turning Point philosophy: Don't be scared. Fear is subjective. If you're not scared, it's not abuse.

During the radio show, Royee Banai responded to Ntoli and basically victim-blamed her. Aubrey Masango, the radio show host, openly stated that in the past he had received plenty of worrying tweets and texts from other 'graduates' reporting similar cases of physical abuse. But then the programme continued down an obtusely un-objective path with little investigation and a lot of chitchat about all the supporters (read: cult-followers).

I believe Ntoli. I was witness to a lot of this torment during my own sittings. When we disobeyed orders, questioned Royee or didn't quite perform as expected, we were screamed at and insulted. Made to feel like lesser human beings.

We were once given an exercise in the early hours of the morning where we had to break our backs by sitting cross-legged on the floor hunched over a couple of matchsticks and some putty to solve a brainteaser. I couldn't do it. Each participant got one of Royee's assistants to help. Helping entailed the assistant sitting next to me and shouting into my left ear. He yelled that I was useless and couldn't do it. Then Royee came over and did the same in my other ear. He called me pathetic until I cried hot tears. No one asked me if I was okay during the break. They couldn't. They were scared and brainwashed by that point. But still, I stayed.

A tired person who is deprived of sleep and food in the middle of the night and has no emotional faculties left will always try to rise above breaking point to prove they are better than they're being told they are. It takes a lot of courage to not care what people think. A lot of energy. When you're hungry and sleep-deprived, you have none of that.

Someone in my workshop also got slapped in the face. Another person was threatened with being kicked out because they challenged Royee on something. Nevertheless, Royee always manipulated us into believing him and believing in the positive effects of his madness. He promised a full refund if we chose to leave. That's how much he believed in the programme, he said. None of us left.

On an online cult forum, a participant said that he ended up walking. He said Royee screamed at his group for eight hours minimum per session. I can testify to this. It happens. This guy couldn't take it any more. He left.

The whole approach of Turning Point is 'break them down to build them up'. First, Royee convinces you that you are a strong human being capable of anything. You are not your experiences. Then he uses the answers you submit on your 'confidential' questionnaire to 'out' you in front of everyone. He offers you opportunities to prove your strength and brainwashes the scepticism out of your system by offering you praise when you 'overcome'. By the end, you're too tired to think critically. You're too tired to think at all. You have become a robot who obeys the master and willingly gives him permission to humiliate you by using your personal experiences against you.

The guy who left did not get his money back. Contrary to the original promise, he was told that the refund was only valid if he had remained in the 'training' for all five days and then decided that it hadn't worked. This reasoning is pretty airtight. By the time five days have passed, most people have followed Royee too far.

I had my third Turning Point breakdown at 4 a.m. one morning when I finally retired to bed after a couple of hours of crawling on my hands and knees from the one end of the hall to the other. I convinced myself that I would have the courage to at least ask for my money back at the end of my five days. I did not.

We ended the workshop the way we participated throughout: with enthusiasm. Because without enthusiasm, we are made to believe, all we have is a self so useless that it is worthy only of death. And we don't want death. Wanting death is what brought us here. We want this amazing, refreshing journey. We *want* this to work. We want a 'new way of life'. We don't want to continue being people so affected by our emotions that we cannot function. So we willingly subject ourselves to the punishment of Turning Point to prove that we are no longer the victims of our experiences, however traumatic, and we can withstand anything. But we can't.

Another caller on the 2014 radio show dialled in to make it clear that we can't withstand just anything. Dr Cathy was her name. She said she had a PhD in clinical psychology. She expressed deep concern about the 'break them down to build them up' technique of Turning Point. Dr Cathy argued that in the face of humiliation, sleep deprivation and physical abuse, defences are down – people break easily and when they do, defences often pop back up in the wrong ways or not at all. That's what I said, Dr Cath!

In a few of the exercises, we were forced to deal with child-hood issues because dealing with cellular memory is a key factor in the coursework. Dr Cathy warned that these kinds of problems, once released – especially under duress – are traumatic and cannot be stitched back together in a healthy way. Not in a few days. And definitely not in a group setting. All accurate.

The 'cellular-memory' portions of the programme were the most destructive to me. In a nutshell, they were emotionally abusive. Or more so than a lot of the other stuff. Each of us would have to sit in the dimly lit hall, again in the wee hours of the morning. An assistant would join us, always dressed in white. They were made to sit and stare at us in silence while we were forced to pretend they were a parent (or both parents, in turns). We had to share all our thoughts about our childhood experiences and upbringing with them. And be honest with them about the destructive role they played in shaping us. If we weren't saying stuff that Royee found satisfactory, he would shout at us again. When I was done, I thought only one thing: this robot in front of me has listened to all my childhood trauma, but I am the one who actually heard it. *Heard it.* I was not ready to hear it. What was I going to do with those memories?

There are many horrific tales out there that far surpass my own experience of that place. A lot of people on forums have shared how they were made to take off their clothes. In fact, on the night of the 2014 radio show, followers started pitching up to the studio in the middle of the night, all of them women in their pyjamas, to support and praise Royee. The host said they were taking their clothes off there as well – in submission. I'm not sure if he was joking or not.

No one took clothes off during my five days. But the 'self-exploration' did leave one feeling naked. And while I am on the subject of nudity, let me point out that many of the themes in Royee's talks were sexual. Sex, infidelity, the way a woman's body (specifically) works, all these things featured. There was a thirteen-year-old girl who was told that if she admitted she was 'wet', she could go up to the stage and Royee would give her a rose. She did. He dismissed the sexual and frankly rapey nature of this with some philosophical gibberish and then complimented her with a full-body hug.

Then, there's the 'cocktail party' where you are reborn after screaming bloody murder and swearing and shouting loud, 'honest' expressions at one another for like two hours to the point of feeling ill. Vomit bags are made available, as are tissues and the like. You can't leave the room. Ever. When you are in there, you are in there. When you are done with the shouting part, it's time for 'rebirth' to the sound of gentle music. The screaming evolves into a sedate saturnalia. Participants are urged to engage in 'cradling'. Everyone admires everyone, everyone is beaming, and some people rock each other back and forth like actual babies.

We were told that everyone who went through this process, including all the other graduates and the drone-like assistants, were now our family. They loved us unconditionally. And there was no way to doubt that, because in the course of those five days, all our dark revelations and vulnerabilities were revealed to them and there they were, cradling us still.

And then, when people were high and hypnotised, everyone participated in the 'gift of giving'. Euphoria is generous. Many cheques with many zeroes were written that night, as donations to the centre. Drugged with persuasion, many participants signed up for the next two courses – Joyspring and The Mile.

This drug of persuasion has many dealers. During my time there I came into contact with a whole bunch of people from all over the world. Some were evangelists and others were proper recruiters. Those who completed The Mile (the last phase) were marked by their white linen clothing. They accepted the training centre's methodology as a way of life and left their home countries to reside in South Africa and live the rest of their lives on the Insight Training Centre property. Why?

When I went to Turning Point, the immune system of my mind was fractured. My culture had no bandage for me. Instead I found refuge in a cult. But cults are the memes of the mental immune system, and memes are viral. When your defences are down, you get infected.

A mind that compromises its mental health in the name of culture is a welcome mat for a pathologically terrible idea.

# My anti-establishment hero, or,
# Grandad, what are you doing?

A lot of things happened in 2004.

At the Hajj pilgrimage in Saudi Arabia 251 people were trampled to death and 244 injured in a stampede.

Kanye West released his debut album, *The College Dropout*. He did not disrupt Taylor Swift on the Grammy stage. 'I'mma let you finish' did not exist yet. He was still of sound mind.

The *New Yorker* published a story with shocking pictures revealing the torture at Abu Ghraib in Iraq, proving that American soldiers had brutalised Iraqis.

Maria Sharapova defeated Serena Williams at Wimbledon – the last time that would ever happen. It was also the only time Sharapova won the ladies' final at the lawn tennis club. We have since learnt that she is the most average player ever and confirmed what we always knew: Serena is the greatest of everything ever.

Roger Federer took his second Wimbledon title. And has since claimed a few more, breaking many records along the way.

Thabo Mbeki was re-elected president of South Africa with an increased majority.

While all this was happening, my grandfather asked that I

submit a piece of writing to him (creative or other) on a weekly basis so he could crit it and give me feedback.

It all started when I got bronchitis that same year. I was on antibiotics the size of horse suppositories and a range of cough syrups. Delirious from fever and drifting in and out of sleep, I heard the bubbles in the Coke Zero on my pedestal start to speak to me. Not in a direct 'Hey Haji, save us, we're trapped in this can' kind of way, but in an indirect narrative kind of way. I started to imagine all sorts of things. At one stage I was in a bubble, floating around in the molasses liquid, trapped but happy. The noise of the story in my head made me jolt out of bed and head for the computer on my desk. Everything I imagined landed up on that page.

For some reason, I printed it out and handed it to my grand-father. He loved it. He told me I was talented and that he wanted me to submit writing to him once a week. Obviously my writing skills faded with the medicated high. The chunk of drivel I submitted next was about culture and reinventing the wheel. He hated it and asked me why I didn't try hard enough. I wanted to tell him it was because the cough syrup was finished and the wheel wasn't at my bedside. When I think about it now, that little tale about a fizzy drink is probably the most embarrass-ing thing I have ever written.

He was an honest guy, my grandfather. A bit left-field with his thoughts, but always honest. His support of my creativity started when I was really young. I spent a lot of time with him at our old house in Laudium. Before I realised I liked writing, I sketched. All the time. He supplied pencils and paper, and I replicated *Secret Seven* book covers.

SABC News was always on in the background and compli-ments for the Indian news presenters spilt out of him. They were all Hindu and he never failed to voice his disappointment and, well, disgust for the Muslim community, who he said never did anything with their lives. 'Baby-making machines,' he called them. 'Will never amount to anything,' he said. He admired women journalists and was frustrated that none of those he saw were Muslim. Subconsciously, I think this played a massive role in my becoming a journalist.

He was a writer too. He wrote poems. Lots and lots of poems. When he wasn't reading them, he was writing them. They were really short, but he took ages to type them because he wasn't used to a computer. He punched each letter in with two fingers and sometimes got the upper- and lower-case letters wrong, resulting in an e.e cummings aesthetic. I assisted with format-ting when asked.

The poems' themes varied from religion to memories of his mother and his childhood. He was never published. Such opportunities did not exist for his generation, class and race. He bought a DIY manual on self-publishing and read it studiously, but nothing came of it. To satisfy his byline needs he got a printer and compiled the poems in files so that they looked like real books. The poetry anthologies of Cassim Mohamed Dawjee are still lying around somewhere in Pretoria.

Reading, writing and watching the news are just about the only conventional things about my grandfather when considered in the light of cultural and religious norms. With every decision, thought and opinion, he proudly lifted his middle finger to the world he found himself in and carved his own path. He didn't care what anyone thought. In that way, he is my hero. He made me laugh without knowing he did. But he also made me think.

Once, when Muslim evangelists pitched up at the gate, he

asked that the dogs be released from the backyard to scare them off. He went outside with a whip to do the same. I love that story.

What follows are a few things my grandfather did in his life, and the lessons I learnt from them.

### Be loyal to your car, but don't give a shit about it

My granddad drove an ancient, massive, olive-green Mercedes-Benz. I don't even know what model it was. It was always falling apart. It was an automatic and it's the car he used to teach me to drive. He was always doing things to the engine that I am pretty sure didn't need doing and only contributed to its demise.

At one stage, the window on the driver's side gave in. It would stay wide open because it just slid right down into the door panel. Instead of having it fixed, Pappie, as we called him, used a butcher's knife to hold it in place. This. Was. A. Terrible. Idea.

He drove me and my sister to school in that car every day. It was a long drive because we lived in Laudium and our school was out of town in Valhalla. He didn't drive well because he always handled the steering wheel with one hand and had his other hand out the window, fingers tapping the roof of the car. In the summer when the whole window thing happened, he'd try to roll the window up and down while driving, constantly dissatisfied with the temperature.

Removing and replacing the knife required him to use both hands. The car went everywhere and so did the massive knife. It was quite a spectacle and quite a chore. The knife needed to be properly rammed into the side of the little window slit, which took some force. He endeavoured to keep his eyes on the road while trying his best not to miss his target and stab himself in the leg. He never missed, and I'm glad about that, but I often find myself laughing to stop from crying with fear of just thinking about it.

*Lesson one: Sometimes in life, all you need is a huge knife to cut through the bullshit. If you believe in yourself, you can always make it work, no matter the risk. And screw the rest.*

## If the puzzle pieces don't fit, throw them away

The June holidays were the longest holidays in the school calendar and Pappie and I always built a puzzle. We started small, 300 pieces or so, and then gradually the puzzles got bigger.

Every day after our 'keep busy' extramural obligations, I would rush home to his dining-room table and admire the progress from the day before. Sometimes, while I was away, he would add more to the puzzle so it was slightly bigger than when I left it. I didn't mind. I am an impatient person and I was keen to see the finished product.

We had a system where he would unpack a variety of porridge bowls and we would sort the pieces before we started. The bits that went on the border were always the easiest to fish out because they all had straight edges, so I went for those first. All of them went into one bowl. Then, we placed the cover of the box in front of us so we could get a feel for the whole picture and start collecting pieces with similar colours that could potentially fit together. Each bowl had a different colour. This process took longer as the pieces got smaller and the puzzles got larger, but we could only start building once we were done doing this. It really was quite a good strategy. Relaxing, too.

One winter holiday we tackled a 5000-piece puzzle. I can't remember what it was, but in my head it's a painting. Possibly a Monet? There were lots of dappled greens and blues, and the details were hard to make out. I think the border bowl was the only one we managed to sort properly that year. This was our Goliath, but I knew the feeling when we were done would be so worth it. That feeling never came.

On a dull, overcast day, I walked to the dining-room table, confident and excited to get started again. As I approached, my steps slowed in confusion: *What is he doing?* Puzzle pieces were strewn everywhere, the bowls empty. Knife in hand (yes, the same one; I think he really liked that knife), he was tearing through the portion of the puzzle we had already managed to construct. Cardboard dust exploded onto the table with each swift slice. In between carving, he gathered the chips of his work into a dinner plate, carried it out to the front garden and littered it onto the sand with flair. Like he was feeding birds or something. Only no one wanted those puzzle pieces, not even him.

I didn't ask him outright what he was doing, but he answered me. 'These pieces don't fit, my child. This puzzle is broken.' In my head I was like, *Uh, yeah. Coz you broke it.*

He added comfortingly, 'Don't worry. We will get one that works and start again.'

*Lesson two: Sometimes in life, you fail. And when you do, fail with passion and then try something new. Don't drive yourself insane with the things you can't do. Try it out, then move on. You can't be great at everything. Admit your weaknesses. Focus on your skill set. And screw the rest.*

## When the neighbours are rowdy, be rowdy too

Laudium was a noisy place. Someone was always revving a stationary car or racing up the road. Kids played in the street while moms yelled at them. Neighbours chatted loudly to each other from the stoep, or shouted at each other across streets. There were constant drive-bys at the house across from ours, where rich youth who'd made their way to the lower parts of town from their mansions on the hills arranged quick drug deals. On Saturdays, there were PAGAD marches to protest against those same drug deals.

Everyone had a dog and at the same time the dogs belonged to no one, so they would bark at each other while patrolling the streets. There was always a broom saleslady yelling *'Besem!'* as she paced the pavements, and doorbells rang constantly as street hawkers carrying bunches of coriander and bouquets of okra on their heads offered their products to housewives. It was vibrant and chaotic. And it came with a soundtrack. More than the revving of engines and the racing of cars was the playing of music.

Men who lived in houses without curtains and looked like they couldn't afford a bath always had cars equipped with the biggest subwoofers. The car across the road was a white Ford Cortina and I am pretty sure I never saw it leave the driveway, but it was packed with more speakers than the FNB Stadium during a sell-out show.

Saturdays and Sundays were particularly noisy. With nothing to do and nowhere to go, the family across the road would mostly hang out in the yard. Dumpies of Black Label and Hansa lined the unfinished brick wall – some full, some empty – while the men took turns walking to the car and back to take a sip and light a cigarette or possibly a joint. Every time they returned to their 'sustenance', the volume on the car stereo would be louder. Now and then a woman would emerge from the front door to empty a dustpan or shake out a rug – but there was never the expected 'Can you please turn that down' conversation.

This was just how days ticked over. The norm. Nothing

unusual. The idea of noise pollution did not exist. The bass rattled the windows of houses to the very end of the street. On Saturday afternoons, the music made my dad's dental practice in the back sound like a house party. At least patients could not be turned off by the frightful buzz of the drill in their mouths. This went on the entire weekend, every single weekend, and not a single soul complained.

Until one fine, sunny Sunday, years after this had been going on, Pappie reached the end of his tether.

My parents, siblings and I lived in the smaller, upstairs section of our house. Even with all the noise outside, we always managed to hear exactly what was going on downstairs. On this particular Sunday, I was sitting on the balcony, watching the white Cortina explode with sound, when my ears caught the hum of a kerfuffle downstairs. My parents were having an afternoon snooze and I was bored out of my mind so I went down to look. In his lounge, my granddad was frantically disconnecting his hi-fi system. It wasn't that big, but it had a lot of wires that connected the small standalone speakers to it. He fussed with this and that, mumbling under his breath.

I assumed my natural position and watched in entertainment. *Hier kom nog 'n ding*, I thought.

He went outside with the equipment bunched up in his arms, wires trailing like streamers, and placed everything on the stairs facing the street. He threaded the cord through the lounge window and hurried inside to plug it in. He had the disposition of a man whose plan was about to come together.

He carried the hi-fi from the stairs with the intention of placing it outside the fence on the curb, but the cord was not long enough. His demeanour changed immediately to one of frustration.

I laughed because this plan was ridiculous: not only was the cord way too short, but the decibels on that system would never compete with the ones in the car. He disappeared. And just when I thought he would give up and the error of his ways was upon him, he returned with an industrial-size extension cord and proceeded to play what I can only remember as the golden oldies on 702. Volume turned up to the max.

He returned to his favourite couch in the lounge, next to the window. The hi-fi remained on the curb, exhaling its death rattle. He settled in, content and proud. He leant back with his eyes closed in meditation and lightly tapped his hands to the beat on the arm of his couch. It was definitely the music of the Cortina he kept rhythm to. His radio was sadly silent in comparison, as I knew it would be. But his little act of revenge drowned out the noise and brought tranquillity to his mind.

*Lesson three: Don't just do something; do something silly. You can't go through the world trying to change anyone, or educate everyone. You don't have to understand everything to accept everything. Sometimes, if you can't beat 'em, join 'em. And screw the rest.*

## Barley soup and ginger beer for the soul

A man of experimentation, my grandfather was. Always taking things apart for no reason to see if he could put them back together again. Sometimes he would intentionally find a problem with something. A button on a cellphone that was too sticky for his liking, a clock mechanism that made too much noise but operated just fine. I think he liked a project. He liked to keep his hands busy.

Once he tore something apart, though, he was mostly unable to get it to function again. His house was always filled with nuts and bolts and discarded wires he never threw away in case he needed them again. In the darkest nooks and crannies, you could find bundles of bits and bobs that all went together to make something that once was and never would be again. He kept all of it. I think he thought the solution would come to him and he would be able to fix it one day. This habit of fiddling with things did not stop with technology or engines or stoves.

Food could not be kept safe from his alchemy either.

Every winter he would make a vegetable soup, heavy with barley, and unintentionally feed the ceiling with it.

He meticulously bought all the ingredients and insisted on boiling everything in a pressure cooker, which always failed him. I'm pretty sure he got the recipe right; the technique, not so much. After it exploded, lid of the pot in the air and soup painted on the ceiling, he would settle for the remnants at the bottom of the pressure cooker – mostly soaked, porridgey barley. He always brought a little over for us to taste in a tiny container. I knew where the rest was, but never said anything. He did this over and over again. Every. Single. Winter. The same meticulous shopping process. The same recipe. The same pot. And the same fail. It was a running winter joke that warmed us in the northern cold.

Then came summer, his ginger beer–brewing season. I can guess at the recipe of the soup, but if you asked me how he made his ginger beer, I would not be able to tell you. I know it had ginger in it – obviously – and yeast. Lots and lots of yeast. He made ginger beer the same way people in the movies make lemonade: habitually. Except he didn't charge five cents per cup. He never got the chance, because, just like the soup exploded in the winter, the ginger beer exploded in the summer, and the only thirst it quenched was that of the hot ceiling above it.

Stained with the silhouette of a cloudy drink, that ceiling was always a reminder of the potential of persistence to leave a mark, which is at least ... something.

*Lesson four: When you bottle things up enough, they're bound to burst out of you, and sometimes that's okay. In the face of adversity, sometimes you just have to say what you have to say. Get angry and empty out the frustration. Leave your mark. And screw the rest.*

### The clock stops short and that's just the way it is

In the winter of 2006, I went to England for three months. I was teaching at an American school so we worked with the US academic calendar, which meant I was treated to a 'spring break' from June to the end of August every year. Paid leave, a decent salary, long holidays and an escape from the winter months. Good deal.

It was my first time abroad alone and I set up base camp in Nottingham with some family and then made my way around the British Midlands. I also spent one day in Edinburgh, where there was no summer but the people were warm.

Close to Nottingham is Derbyshire, where you will find the house of D.H. Lawrence. My grandfather loved D.H. Lawrence, and *The White Peacock* was one of his favourite books. He reread it so many times the pages of his copy were worn thin by their turning. He also loved a woman in Birmingham, which isn't too far from Nottingham either.

I must have been a year or two old when this woman stayed with us. It was soon after my grandmother died, and I think it gave him some peace to have this companion. She ended up leaving for England, where she would receive better support and an education for her son, who suffered from a mental illness. She

185

and my grandfather never saw each other again. But they loved each other through flowers, birthday cards and long letters, year after year.

Her letters were typical of the ones I saw in films: rhythmic cursive on light-blue paper and wrapped in envelopes bordered by dark-blue and red candy stripes. They were foreign to me, and I romanticised their aesthetic without ever reading the letters. They were stamped with the seal of the queen and I remember thinking it was very special to receive something like that in the mail, even though the correspondence was not for me.

Sometimes they called each other. Once she called late at night and, knowing it was she, he rushed to the phone, barefoot in the dark, feeling for the landline's receiver. The next day he had an untidy plaster wrapped around the toe he'd stubbed on the couch. I have no idea what they talked about, but I knew they had a lot to say.

My grandmother died when I was nine months old, but I feel like I have some weird connection to her. Bloodlines, I guess. For this woman, besides being enchanted by her stamps and her envelopes, I felt nothing.

Before I left for England, Pappie called me to his place (which was just through the garage of ours at our new home). He asked me to sit down and handed me a piece of paper with an address and a telephone number. He asked me sweetly to please find the time and a way to see her when I was in England. 'Tell her I still think about her. And my child, if you do this for me, I will die a happy man.'

I bought chocolates and a bunch of flowers and went to the flat where she lived with her son. I called beforehand to explain who I was and who was sending me. When I walked into her house, the first thing I noticed was a green couch. It was very similar to my grandfather's favourite single-seater. It's like they sat in the same chair, miles apart. The second thing I noticed was a framed picture of the Aga Khan on her wall. The third thing was how tiny that flat was. I am short, but it made me feel big. Sadness fell over me. I was glad I'd come, but I felt weak and I still don't know why.

Her son brought in a bowl of ice cream. He was about forty and doing well. He had a part-time job at a grocery store. She looked nothing like the pictures I remembered. The Sophia Loren look from the sepia photographs my grandfather had shown me had undergone a metamorphosis and become a sharp but underexposed image of a woman battered by age. We made small talk. I had no idea what to ask, what to say. She asked about my mother and father. She did not mention my grandfather yet, at all. I started to get the feeling I had imagined their whole relationship and that I had made the closeness of them up. I kept reminding myself why I was there in the first place.

She asked me about my life. Reminded me of when last she'd seen me and said I had grown into a beautiful young woman. The awkward silence was filled with passing around the box of chocolates I brought with me. I started to panic. And then the question came.

'How is your grandfather?'

I told her exactly what I had to. I left out the part about him dying a happy man if I delivered the message. Then I thanked her for the ice cream and made my way out. She stopped me at the door and fetched an envelope. 'Give this to him,' she said.

I placed the note in the new copy of *The White Peacock* I had purchased from the D.H. Lawrence museum and tucked it away in my backpack so it wouldn't crease.

I made my way home in the beginning of August, and as soon

as I got home I handed it to Pappie. He opened the book, held the envelope and smiled. He didn't ask how she was. He just looked at me and said: 'Thank you my child. Now... I can die a happy man.'

My grandfather died the next month.

*Lesson five: You die the way you live, on your own terms. And... screw the rest.*

# Sorry, not sorry

One afternoon in the autumn of 2014, I took a mannerly stroll in Parkhurst with a colleague. We ended up in the dog park we frequented. It's a well-known park in the area and the residents of the suburb convene there to end the workday. People are desperate for this kind of leisure activity in Joburg, where they're starved of accessible public spaces. Outdoor experiences are few and far between unless you're willing to drive for a while. Like maybe to the next province, which is not possible during the week.

On this particular day, I took my place on a park bench before peak home-time and my mind brain-farted in a big way. The park was filled with domestic workers looking after other people's kids. I felt a bit nauseous. I had been to the park at a later hour before, when the parents took the place of their domestic workers and the park was bleached by the property owners, contrasted only with the colours of their dogs' coats.

Grappling with all this, I wrote a column for the *Mail & Guardian* the next day, about the plight of domestic workers in South Africa. The title was 'Maid in South Africa'. The blurb: 'White people can walk their dogs in South Africa, but not their children.'

It did not go down well. Community boards filled up with anti-Haji messages. Residents who received the local newsletter were warned about my presence at the park and the casting of my 'evil' eye. The guns of white liberals were fully loaded with white tears and they guarded their privilege with shields made of worn defences. Local bloggers with big mouths and little to say shared the column only to castigate me. The same colleague warned me to never return to the park. Her value severely diminished after this warning. There was an ongoing attempt to ban me from a public space. Such is the delusional capacity of a closed-minded and cushioned society. Hilarious really.

Then, the worst happened. In an attempt to calm the 'masses', this colleague who had accompanied me that day came to my 'rescue'. She insisted on writing a response disguised as a defence against my controversial opinion. This bugged me. A lot. Her wanting to jump on the bandwagon did not surprise me, but it was her motivation for wanting to write the piece that bugged me – the saviour complex. Still, I couldn't quite put my finger on the massive irritation it stirred in me.

After some discussion with friends it became blatantly clear: she needed to whitesplain. She needed to whitesplain my thoughts and sanitise them with her 'wokeness'. I had spoken at her people. She needed to speak *with* them. The title of her piece? 'There's *more* to getting maid in South Africa'. And just after the head-line she launched in to 'please explain' the brown girl in the ring of white fire.

'Last week a group of *Mail & Guardian* readers rallied around to rage at a column published by Haji Mohamed Dawjee,' the piece began. Then she threw me a bone: 'The column makes qualified statements that the white people of Johannesburg's leafy suburb of Parkhurst might be delegating child-minding to domestic workers so that they are freed up to walk their dogs. It also suggests that child-minding might be a duty that the domestic workers had not agreed to.' She reminded her people that 'Mohamed Dawjee's commentary elicited a fireworks display of fury'.

And then, most significantly, she threw *her* people a bone: 'Because I am not a mother, I cannot know exactly what I will decide about who looks after my child one day. But I do know that I would probably feel as angry as many of these readers if someone questioned my decision about this without knowing my reasons.'

I am sure those who 'raged' against my column slept easy the night they read the above piece. I, however, did not. It was condescending. The whole thing was condescending. But because of my conditioning – brought to you by the colour of my skin and years of taming – I said nothing. I might even have called the piece 'good' at some point. But time brought to the surface the regularity of occurrences like this. I started to take stock of the same denigration by the same person, over and over again in different ways. And then I started seeing it in other young white people as well. A select number raised on smoothies made of wokeness and little else. It was a club. Its members were people who thought they were acting with the best of intentions, but who were completely deaf to the patronising quality of their acts.

That white colleague's need to write a follow-up to my column was yet another silencing of sorts. Another way for a privileged white to hijack the conversation in the name of 'good'.

This tore at me for a long time. I regretted not saying enough. Not standing up for myself enough. I regretted playing into the hands of white sensitivities and being careful not to hurt this person's feelings. I put myself second.

Eventually I realised that the art of apology had become exhausting. More than that, it had become insincere. *What is this nonsense,* I thought, *of people of colour (women especially) always needing to be the bigger person by making themselves small?* And so the seed of the following statement was planted.

## THE SORRY, NOT SORRY MANIFESTO

*I believe...*
In bursting the bubble. I believe in confidently crossing the imaginary line of what is okay to say to white people and what is not. I believe that it is our turn to talk and their turn to listen. If they won't, it is often going to be my responsibility to tell them to shut up. At the same time, I believe in picking my battles. Not everyone is worthy of my time and investment. I believe that I am entitled to the silence of my choosing because I do not have to be a representative for an entire demographic and I do not have to explain that demographic as an individual. I have had my fair share of white tears and I no longer thirst for them.

*I will contribute to a world where...*
People are no longer allowed to live in spaces defined only by *their* wants and needs. I will contribute by making this clear through conversation and opinion in order to expose these very people to the short-sightedness of their own making.

I will contribute to a world where our unreal, unrecognised feelings are made real by troubling the status quo of privilege and encouraging a critical discussion on race. I will contribute to a world where white liberals are forced out of their homogeneous comfort zones and into a place of self-reflection and fault-seeking.

I will contribute to a world where those very liberals are no longer allowed to romanticise other cultures and races just because they advocate for charities or NGOs or any other civil rights movements.

I will contribute to a world where the comfortable are disturbed. Where it is not only the oppressed who are targeted (and who often target themselves, as I have done). I will contribute to a world where the white person, regardless of generation, is forced to accept and understand their belonging to the class of the oppressor. I will rattle the cages of the content and comfort the concerned.

I will contribute to a world that no longer accepts that confidence is a ticket purchased by privilege and race, giving these people a free ride to the podium and the power to speak, often without script, about the issues that belong to us ... to me.

I will contribute to a world where the woke white is aware that wokeness is often selfish. It is a cloak made of personal gain – whether socially or politically – and the thread of insight is often lacking. I will contribute to a world where the status of this woke white does not give them permission to act as saviours to the 'less fortunate' so that they can feel righteous and exceptional, thereby consoling themselves.

I will contribute to a world where I too can make myself rich with the fortunes of confidence.

*Here's what I know for sure:*
There is a good racist and there is a bad racist.

I prefer the latter. The latter wears his or her spots proudly and is easier to identify.

193

The good racist is work.

The good racist, when accused of racism, is shielded by their identification as an anti-racist. When confronted by accusations of racism, however subtly these acts are practised, the good racist resorts to tears.

Tears are work and I know for sure that I will no longer be providing the tissues to wipe up this degree of self-pity. This is not my job. Nor is it my job to act like I am invisible.

I know for sure that I will change my approach. I will no longer hang around silently while the audible voices around me hold a forum on their 'useful' contributions.

I know for sure that it is both okay and useful for the woke white to struggle with their own conscience. To feel guilt, fear, doubt and self-castigation. I know for sure that this is healthy and any contribution I make to doctor this situation and treat them as victims is not healing at all. It perpetuates the problem.

The good racist is work, but the good racist is not my job. The good racist is the good racist's problem and I will no longer contribute to fixing or healing them without having done the same for myself first.

I know for sure that white privilege and racism have taught me that I am not entitled to my own feelings and opinions. I know for sure that they have built a world in which they have plenty of space and I am entitled to very little.

I know for sure that my thoughts and ideas have existed without consideration, yet in this world I have been taught to consider the feelings of others.

I know for sure that my socialisation in this world has been defined by shutting up, hiding who I really am, staying out of the way and being grateful for being allowed to even exist in certain spaces. I know for sure that this stops now.

I know for sure that those who are protected by their own liberal ideologies struggle to listen to voices that they do not identify with – even if this is not obvious to them.

I know for sure that when they enter a racially diverse room, they immediately divide the area into the haves and the have-nots without even thinking about it. They know that they are among the haves, and duty-bound to show charity to the have-nots. It is true that there are those with privilege and those without, but by categorising the world in this way and positioning themselves as saviours, these liberals exert their privilege to survive a changing system that is threatening to them.

*Here's how I know what I know for sure:*
I have witnessed the capturing of conversations about diversity, political correctness or any kind of human right. I have seen white liberals appropriate the conversation and decide what is worthy of outrage and what isn't.

I have seen them slyly slip from one side when speaking through powerful structures like the media, to the other at casual closed-circle storytelling around a braai. The changing of teams is a regular occurrence in safe environments: I have seen this side-swap occur as a means to a racist end, or as a tragic stab at curt humour.

I have been irritated by the giddy reactions of woke whites when they are confronted with the injustices committed by members of their own race who they deem 'less enlightened' than they are. The bad whites vs the good whites. But I have realised that there is one ring that binds them, so to speak, and that is their contribution to a reality that is actually quite fucked. A reality they have the power to escape at any time. I have realised that not all of them have accepted this truth.

I know what I know for sure because I am real. I am a person who has, like so many others, been subjected to a world where white feelings flooded my own. Who has been convinced, systemically, that being a person of colour is only torture and suffering. As a child, this was beyond my comprehension. It split my mind in two with a trauma that still rears its ugly head every now and then because I continue to live in a system where I need, in many ways, to survive before I can just thrive.

## Conclusion

I am not sorry about refusing to prioritise white feelings when it comes to conversations about structural racism.

I am not sorry about the fact that you do not want to hear me. Your denial is *your* baggage and it will not stop me from raising my voice.

I am not sorry that my raised voice offends you or that you suffer an emotional disconnect because of it. There has always been one, and I won't feel sorry for you if you have not realised this yet.

I will not be sorry for making it known to you that it is impossible for you to fully embrace me, a person of colour, as an equal whose feelings are as valid as your own because you still operate under an umbrella of privilege that holds your own emotions in higher regard than anyone else's – whether you realise it or not. To fully embrace me you must acknowledge this and believe it.

I am not sorry that the above is confusing to you. And I am not sorry about the pain that confusion brings.

I am not sorry about the fact that I will no longer be a gymnast cartwheeling around my words and thinking about what the right and wrong thing is to say in order to succeed in piercing through your denial of the politics of race.

I am not sorry that our experiences of race come from a different place. When we engage in conversation about it, I won't be sorry for saying that it is impossible for your opinion to carry any weight, regardless of how much amplification your liberalness buys you. You cannot have an opinion on the details of a problem that does not affect you personally. We are not equals in the fight to end discrimination. I am not sorry that in this type of engagement, you are the lesser, the ill-equipped.

I am not sorry that your rainbow nation did not work out. That you have tried your best to be a nice white person and you feel cheated by your efforts, because you cannot see that your disappointment in the lack of fruition of said rainbow nation lacks empathy. I am not sorry that you feel silenced. I am not sorry for this, because your feeling silenced slaps the faces of those who have been silenced for far too long. Check yourself.

I am not sorry that my truth offends you. Even if you are a good person. My truth has faced consequences and it will face consequences still. When you speak the same truth you are seen as a hero among your people, while your silence is a way to get ahead in life. Your preachy wisdom on diversity is a way to get ahead in life as well. It's all win-win. I am not sorry that I will question this almost genetic entitlement without once again tiptoeing around your feelings so as not to implicate you personally. A structure has many parts. You are one of them. I am not sorry about that.

I am not sorry that I refuse to let you exercise said entitlement towards me. You are not entitled to my time, my energy, my efforts; I am in control of that. Exercising this control does not mean that I will change this white world, but at least I can tip the scales in my favour.

I am not sorry that I will no longer ignore racial, economic and social segregation and the psychological effects it has had on me in exchange for 'making it' in your world.

I am not sorry that I will no longer justify my right to have nice things in letters of apology penned in pain.

I am not sorry that it is not my job to liberate you from the chains of privilege, from the prison of your collective thought. And I am not sorry that it is your responsibility to come to terms with the oppression that accompanies privilege – the oppression that your liberal mind inflicts on you, shaped as it is by institutions and practices that, at the heart of it all, are divisive and exploitative. The onus is on you to come to terms with that.

I am not sorry that I question you, that I doubt you, that I think *you* are different and that, sometimes, I think you are dangerous. I am not sorry that I am no longer afraid.

Sorry, but I am not sorry.

# Acknowledgements

To my parents, Professor Salahuddien Mohamed Dawjee and Ghyroonnisha Dawjee. Thank you for your patience, your guidance, and for skelling me, without which there would be no fire in me and no flames to throw.

To my siblings, Dr Maryam Dawjee and Muhammad Dawjee. Thank you for always being an endless supply of inspiration and for taking care of me. Thank you for advising me to never carry a handbag because I always leave it in restaurants. Thank you for giving me the comfort of knowing that whatever else I am not, I am at least the older sibling to two of the world's smartest, kindest and most beautiful human beings.

To Paps, who likes to give books away – I wrote this one just so that you would be obligated to keep it. May its existence annoy you from your bookshelf for years to come. I win.

To my mentors: Hannelie Booyens, once my lecturer and now my friend, who said about my writing, 'There's a place for your sarcastic fucked-up-ness somewhere in the world.' Hannelie, I think I have found that place. To Susan Booyens, for endless conversations about annoying Afrikaans people. And, finally,

to Chris Roper, who gave me my first column at the *Mail &
Guardian*. I thank you, and I apologise for the troubles.

To Ferial Haffajee, whom I contacted in 2010 for a job. She
advised me to get a qualification in journalism first and then forgot about me – a random, weird stranger. Years later, Ms Haffajee
would refer to me as part of a 'new world order' in her book,
*What If There Were No Whites in South Africa?* Okay, I don't
know if that is the exact quote, but I am mentioned (along with
a host of other, much cooler people). Thank you for writing the
foreword; your hero, Haji.

To my squads: the Nyak Squad, the Bean Club and the Papses
– specifically Stephanie Pekeur, my Raym-drops and Sarah
Koopman. Thank you for being the best friends and the best
fans anyone could ever ask for. Whatsapp me, okay?

To Garreth van Niekerk, thank you for reminding me to cut
my hair when it looks *kak*. But mostly, thank you for being so
wonderfully you.

To my soul-friend, Rasheda Titus. Thank you for buying me
that pen once upon a time to write this book. Writing by hand
makes for bad cramps. But here we are.

Thank you to my team at Penguin Random House: Robert
Plummer, Marlene Fryer and Melt Myburgh. Mostly, thank
you to my editor, Lauren Smith. I'm so glad we finally had that
coffee so that I could thank you in person.

To the person responsible for making me look marvellous on
the cover of this book, Neo Baepi. I cannot thank you enough;
the words have not been invented yet.

To Charlie, our cat. Thank you for your paw-fect contributions in the way of typos and computer reboots. Hope you're
resting well and making 'em laugh up there, puppy bear.

And to my wife, Rebecca Davis, without whom this book

would have been completed with a calm sense of control instead of anxiety, haste and a lot of playtime. I would not have it any other way. Thank you for helping me eat the elephant, not one bite at a time, but by dipping its trunk in wasabi. I love you.

HAJI MOHAMED DAWJEE
CAPE TOWN, FEBRUARY 2018

# Notes and references

## We don't really write what we like
p. 2 'the most potent weapon ...': Steve Biko, *I Write What I Like*
(digital edn, Chicago: University of Chicago Press, 1978), p. 74.
p. 3 'So as a prelude ...': Ibid.

## Begging to be white?
p. 37 'Race doesn't really exist for you ...': Chimamanda Ngozi
Adichie, *Americanah* (USA: Alfred A. Knopf, 2013), p. 429.

## And how the women of Islam did slay
p. 49 **Bibi**: Arabic feminine title of honour and rank.
p. 49 **Women Kurdish soldiers are the best ISIS deterrents**: Norma
Costello, 'Isis in Iraq: The female fighters that strike fear into
Jihadis – because they'll rob them of paradise', *Independent*,
10 April 2016, http://www.independent.co.uk/news/world/
middle-east/isis-in-iraq-the-women-kurd-and-yazidi-fighters-
that-put-the-fear-into-jihadis-because-theyll-rob-a6977761.html,
last accessed January 2018.
p. 56 'Islam is a religion where your temple is not a building ...':
International Association of Sufism, http://ias.org/sufism/
women-in-islam/, last accessed January 2018.

### Why I'm down with *Downton Abbey*

p. 97 **Reasons why *Downton Abbey* is so good**: Brian Moylan, 'Why everyone in the universe should watch *Downton Abbey*', *Gawker*, 9 January 2012, http://gawker.com/5874387/why-everyone-in-the-universe-should-watch-downton-abbey, last accessed January 2018.

p. 99 **Race-based trauma is a 'natural byproduct ...'**: Monnica Williams, interviewed by Jenna Wortham in 'Racism's psychological toll', *New York Times*, 24 June 2015, https://www.nytimes.com/2015/06/24/magazine/racisms-psychological-toll.html, last accessed January 2018.

p. 101 **'White people hold the power ...'**: James Baldwin, 'Letter from a region in my mind', *The New Yorker*, 17 November 1962, https://www.newyorker.com/magazine/1962/11/17/letter-from-a-region-in-my-mind, last accessed January 2018.

### My mother, the true radical

p. 118 **It lacked 'substance'**: Christina Cauterucci, 'Jennifer Lopez's new video is a sad premonition of the future of feminism', *Slate*, 6 May 2016, http://www.slate.com/blogs/xx_factor/2016/05/06/jennifer_lopez_s_new_ain_t_your_mama_video_is_a_sad_premonition_of_the_future.html, last accessed January 2018.

### A better life with Bollywood

p. 134 **'I feel I have gone back in past'**: Lata Mangeshkar, as quoted in The Rediff Interview with Yash Chopra, *Rediff*, 14 September 2004, http://www.rediff.com/movies/2004/sep/14yash.htm, last accessed January 2018.

### Joining a cult is a terrible idea

p. 164 **Turning Point workshop**: Insight Training Centre website, http://www.insighttc.co.za/index.php/the-workshops/stage-1-turning-point, last accessed January 2018.

p. 166 **Royee Banai bio**: Insight Training Centre website, http://www.insighttc.co.za/index.php/about-us/trainer-royee-banai, last accessed January 2018.